Creating your Vintage
HALLOWE'EN

Creating your Vintage

HALLOWE'EN

The folklore, traditions, and some crafty makes

MARION PAULL

CICO BOOKS

LONDON NEW YORK

Published in 2014 by CICO Books
an imprint of Ryland Peters & Small Ltd
20–21 Jockey's Fields, London WC1R 4BW
519 Broadway, 5th Floor, New York, NY 10012

www.rylandpeters.com

10 9 8 7 6 5 4 3 2 1

Text © Marion Paull 2014
Project text © Emma Hardy
Recipe text © Heather Cameron
Design and photography © CICO Books 2014

Illustrations on pages 1–3, 7, 12, 15, 18, 20, 25, 29,
31, 37, 42, 45, 65, 68–69, 75, 79–80, 82–83, 87–88, 98,
102–103, 107–109, 111, 121, 123–124, 133 © Corbis

A CIP catalog record for this book is available from
the Library of Congress and the British Library.

ISBN: 978-1-78249-143-9

Designer: Mark Latter
Project photographs: Debbie Patterson
Recipe photograph: Heather Cameron
Step-by-step illustrations: Harriet de Winton

Printed in China

9001093260

CONTENTS

INTRODUCTION

Hallowe'en has never been more popular—trick-or-treating, dressing up, parades, themed parties. The old festival is enjoying a revival in the UK and Europe, and in America, billions of dollars are spent each year on costumes, decorations, party goods, party food, pumpkins, and, of course, candy. Go back a hundred and more years, and most of those things were homemade. Innovation and imagination were given free rein and it didn't really matter if the results were glitzy or homey. The preparations were all part of it. Hallowe'en was a fabulous excuse for a party.

By the mid-19th century, the old Hallowe'en festival had mostly faded into obscurity, localized even in the Celtic regions of the UK—Ireland, Scotland, Wales, the Isle of Man, and the West country—as well as northern England, until with mass immigration into America, it started to capture the collective imagination Stateside. Within a few generations, Hallowe'en had been transformed from a collection of slightly quirky, regional rituals into a community get-together, a family-fun day. Observance and customs developed along regional lines, but the universal overall theme was the same—it was happy fairytale time, despite a certain boisterousness with pranks and practical jokes, made all the better for the frisson of a little extra spookiness and an element of daring to be frightened (although you knew, with your sensible head on, that there was absolutely nothing to be frightened of!)

Just as much a part of an old-fashioned Hallowe'en as the costumes, decorations, and Jack o' lanterns were the fortune-telling

games, which were indispensable to the night's entertainment. Of course, none of the charms was ever guaranteed to work. In fact, they were not really expected to provide accurate predictions of the future, but it was fun to have a go and to follow the old traditions. They were all part of the amusements for an annual occasion that was—and still is—quite different from any other.

In these sophisticated, high-tech days of rampant commercialization, looking back to simpler times has an undeniable appeal, and enthusiasm for all things vintage could hardly leave out one of fall's main events. Hallowe'en continues to be celebrated with such gusto and commitment because it changes with the times, but sometimes it's great to rewind and discover how things were done in your grandparents' and great-grandparents' day. It's also oddly heartening to know that, even in this modern age when everything changes with bewildering speed, vague links with an older time can still be traced, and vestiges of even older ways may have survived.

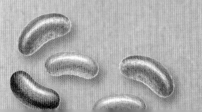

7

When clouds appear, wise men put on their cloaks;
When great leaves fall, the winter is at hand;
When the sun sets, who doth not look for night?

Richard III by William Shakespeare

chapter 1

WAY
BACK WHEN...

Way back when...

"The days are getting shorter. The warmth is going out of the sun. The cattle have been brought down from their high summer pastures and the crops are safely stored. Soon the great fires will be lit to mark the end of the old year and the start of the new. The Dark Year is nearly upon us. Are we well enough prepared?"

Perhaps something like this was going through the minds of the Celtic tribes of northern Europe at the end of what we know as October, two thousand and more years ago. For the Celts, life was divided seasonally in a constant round of death and renewal. Winter was the start of a new cycle, a dark time of cold and hunger if not enough food had been stored, a time to be wary, hunker down, and concentrate on getting through until the warm sunlight returned, as it surely would.

The changing seasons were of vital importance when people provided their own food and shelter—no driving down to the store to pick up any forgotten groceries or calling the handyman to fix the roof—and they were faithfully observed with rituals and festivals. The Celts lived close to nature,

and it shaped their beliefs. Specific times in the year were celebrated to honor and possibly placate the gods, and encourage the deities to look favorably on the Earth and its people. The longest and shortest days (solstices) and the two occasions when day and night are of equal length (equinoxes) were obvious markers, but the four changes of season had just as much if not more significance. These were marked with fire festivals, celebrations of life and connection to Earth—Samhain (November 1), Imbolc (February 1), Beltain (May 1), and Lughnasadh (August 1). These are today's dates. Back then, the actual day would have depended on the cycle of the moon, but the parties started on the preceding evening since the Celts thought of day following night, rather than the other way around. The festival of Samhain (pronounced Sah-wen),

A MERRY HALLOWEEN

which marked the end of summer and the onset of winter, is thought by many people to be the origin of Hallowe'en.

What we know of these festivals is based mainly on myths and legends, stories passed down through generations by word of mouth before being written down hundreds of years later. Factual evidence is hard to come by. Descriptions of rituals and beliefs are, necessarily, to a great extent fanciful and, inevitably, interpretations, suppositions, and well-educated guesses have been added through the ages. However, some archaeological evidence does exist and suggests that in Ireland at least, two thousand and more years ago, great fires burned at the Hill of Ward, or Tlachtga, in County Meath. We can probably assume that fires of such size were of significance to the people, and if here, so one argument goes, why not in the other Celtic lands of northern Europe? Remains of a prehistoric hillfort have been unearthed at Tlachtga, and legend has it that this was a gathering place for the Druids, who were Celtic priests and leaders.

The Hill of Tara

References in medieval texts suggest that at Samhain a feast was held at Tara that went on for six or seven days. A well-known Irish heritage site, Tara is the location of many mythological tales. This was where the Irish High King kept court and warrior bands, the Fianna, gathered. In one story, the land had once belonged to the fairies, who had been chased from it by mankind, and they were not happy about it! Every year for twenty-three years, Aillen, a fairy prince, would turn up at Samhain and send everyone to sleep with his wonderful music. Then he would burn the palace to the ground. No one was ever hurt but the palace was reduced to ashes and every year it was rebuilt. Inevitably, a superhero came along. Fionn, son of a former leader of the Fianna, kept himself from succumbing to the magical music by the rather drastic measure of jabbing his spear into his forehead, and then killing Aillen with the same spear. Fionn was acclaimed leader of the Fianna and went on to save the day many times throughout Ireland and Scotland.

FIRE

In Celtic folklore, fire was thought of as cleansing as well as symbolizing strength and passion, and fire festivals seem to have been an intrinsic part of Celtic ritual. According to tradition, a few crops and the bones of slaughtered animals were thrown on the Samhain fires as offerings to powerful gods. Sometimes, two bonfires were lit and the livestock was driven between them to purify the animals and give them a chance of surviving the winter months. Those chosen for slaughter—generally the older, weaker animals—would be killed, their meat preserved, and the bones burnt (the word bonfire comes from bone-fire).

Everyone would let their home fire die down and rekindle it from the ashes of the big fires for good luck during the coming darkness. Winter was trouble enough without storing up more by not taking every opportunity to propitiate the gods. The remaining ashes were spread over the fields to guard against evil spirits causing the failure of next year's crop—and also the ash was a good fertilizer. In Scotland,

young men would run around the fields carrying flaming torches, to protect the land from any malevolent forces that may have been lurking in the vicinity. Bonfires continued to be lit at Hallowe'en in Celtic regions over the centuries. Even today, in many areas of Scotland, the new year is celebrated with bonfires. That may be December 31 in the modern calendar, but back in the day, Celtic new year was October 31. It may be too fanciful to see a link, but it's an appealing idea—and in at least one place, Fortingall, a huge Samhain bonfire was lit each year, albeit on November 11, right up until 1924.

Hallowe'en bonfires are still traditional in Ireland, although the authorities are trying to discourage them because of the fire risk. In Wales, the Samhain bonfire was known as Coel Coeth and there, as in Ireland and elsewhere, it was considered good luck to jump over the dying flames (maybe because it would be pretty bad luck if you didn't make it!). In the old days, young people would lie down next to the fires so that the smoke wafted over them, perhaps originally to ward off evil spirits but later probably because it was quite a daring thing to do, and if one person did it, why not join in?

Roaming spirits

Some say that Samhain was also known as the Festival of the Dead. On this night, those who had died during the year crossed to the Otherworld, and relatives would leave out food and drink and keep candles burning to help them on their way. Another tale was that the division between this world and the next became wispy and fragile. Spirits would pass through on their way to revisit their earthly haunts, and the food and drink and candles were to welcome them home, if just for a short while.

When the Romans began to dominate Celtic lands, a harvest festival for their goddess of fruitfulness, Pomona, took place in the fall, and some say this became confused with Samhain, but others maintain that the two remained separate. The Romans finally conquered Britain in 43 CE, but they never ventured as far north as Scotland or across into Ireland. However, Pomona's symbol is an apple—she is often portrayed wearing a circlet of apples on her head, and that fruit has remained firmly associated with Hallowe'en to this day.

Fairies and nature spirits were also out and about at Samhain, and the spirits of those who were seeking revenge for wrongs done to them in life. Portals would open by burial mounds and fairy sites. Strangers were treated with respect. They could be spirits in disguise, malevolent or otherwise, and since there was no way of knowing, it was deemed unwise to offend them—better to welcome them and offer hospitality in the form of shelter, food, and drink. In any case, benign spirits were to be encouraged. They were thought to help the Druids make predictions about the coming winter, possibly offering some hope in what must have seemed a long and comfortless time.

The action takes place at Cruachan, now Rathcroghan, which is another well-known heritage site, redolent with mystical tales and magical associations. King Ailill and Queen Maeve are holding a feast for Samhain. The king has issued a challenge—to go to a gallows where two criminals have been hanged and tie a twig around the ankle of one of the corpses. Several have tried and failed, beaten back by their fear of the demons and spirits that haunt the land on this night.

One fearless young man, Nera, takes the challenge and is promised the king's gold-hilted sword as reward if he succeeds. At the gallows, he ties the twig as bidden and, this being Samhain when the dead are able to return to Earth, the dead man asks him for a drink. Nera takes the man on his back, eventually finds someone willing to provide water—although it takes three attempts, which is not really surprising, considering this gallant young man is carrying a reviving corpse!—and then

returns him to the gallows. When he gets back to the royal court to claim his reward, he finds it in flames and everyone killed. Nera follows a fairy host into the Hill of Cruachan—a fairy stronghold—where he meets a woman who tells him that he has seen a vision of what will happen next Samhain unless he forewarns his masters and comrades. Nera goes back to tell Ailill, Maeve, and the people of Cruachan of the danger, taking some summer flowers from the fairies' haven to prove that what he is telling them is true. In some versions of the story he stays a year in company with the fairy woman before returning to tip off his mortal chums; in others he goes back sooner and then escapes with her before Ailill and Maeve attack the Hill of Cruachan and destroy it. Either way, he seems to have done his duty and got the girl.

Hallowmas

Once Christianity arrived—it was legalized throughout the Roman Empire in 313 CE—all sorts of interesting things happened to pagan festivals.

The old ways were deeply rooted and not easily abandoned. Whether through belief in the supernatural, faith in the power of ritual, or just a love of tradition, the fall fire festival continued to be observed as a time of closeness to the Otherworld and the spirits of loved ones who had passed on, and of divination. In 601 CE, Pope Gregory, in an effort to wean local people away from their old beliefs, instructed his missionaries to take over local customs and religious sites, rather than banning and destroying them, and adapt them to the Church's purpose. The ancient deities were named as demons, though, and their priests reviled as evil representatives of the Devil. But through the following centuries it remained hard to dislodge the notion that, either on that one particular night or the next each year, the dead came back to visit and the living had better be prepared.

In Rome in 609 CE, the Emperor Phocas gave the Pantheon to Pope Boniface IV and on May 13 he dedicated it to St Mary and All Martyrs. There had been plenty of them under the old Roman rule—too many for each one to be allocated a separate day. So it became the custom for all the saints and martyrs who didn't have a specific day of their own to be honored together on one day, All Hallows' Day (hallow means holy). In Rome, after the dedication of the church, this was May 13, but it was observed at different times all over Europe. A hundred or so years later, Pope Gregory III moved the date from May 13, declaring November 1 to be the Feast of All Saints in Rome, and, in the ninth century, Pope Gregory IV nominated November 1 as the universal date for the Western Church. (Eastern Orthodox Churches continue to observe All Saints' Day in the spring, on the first Sunday after Pentecost.) Some historians believe the date was chosen deliberately to supersede pagan fall festivals, while others say it was merely coincidental. Likewise, the remembrance of all martyrs on May 13 had coincided with the pagan observance of Lemuria, on

Danse macabre

In medieval times, all over Europe the danse macabre was a tool for emphasizing the inevitability of death, whatever your station in life. In plays put on in churches, monasteries, cemeteries, and probably mansions and palaces, the figure of death led a cross section of the living, from king to laborer, toward their inescapable end. Depictions of the danse macabre appeared on church and monastery walls. Plays and wall paintings were among the main ways for priests to get their message across to a congregation, most of whom could neither read nor write. The danse macabre reminded everyone of the shortness of life, and the priest would be on hand to reinforce the message that, bearing in mind what might be to come, being good was preferable to being sinful.

In some places, children dressed up as characters from the danse macabre while keeping vigil on All Hallows' Eve.

which day the restless spirits of the dead were mollified.

Coming on for two hundred years later, Abbot Odilo of Cluny (who died in 1049) declared that November 2 would be set aside to pray for the souls of the departed, languishing in purgatory. All Souls' Day, marked by the ringing of church bells, would follow All Saints' Day—maybe since the belief was that saints could intercede on behalf of the dead—making it a two-day festival. This was known as Hallowmas or Hallowtide, and it started, often with a vigil, the previous evening, All Hallows' Eve. That's a short step to Hallowe'en, and almost certainly the origin of the name, but whether what we know as Hallowe'en is an evolution of early Christian practices or of an ancient Celtic ritual, or neither, is open to conjecture. The truth is that no one knows for sure.

On All Souls' Eve (November 1), many people burned candles to guide the souls of their dear departed back to visit their earthly homes, and put out a glass of wine for them (in much the same way as legend has it the Celts did on Samhain). However, ideas were gradually changing and, particularly after the Reformation in the 16th century (which resulted in the establishment of the Protestant church), any wandering spirits of the dead returned

to Earth were often deemed to be of malicious intent rather than the souls of loving friends and relatives making contact with comforting messages. They were denounced as witches and demons, and some people put out food and drink, not to attract them but rather to persuade these threatening beings to do no harm. Others concentrated on candlelit processions, ringing church bells, and blessing homes, harvested corn, and livestock to protect them from the forces of evil.

Tonight, if true the legend tells,
All parted souls return;
When softly toll the midnight bells
And red the hearth-fires burn,
The wistful sprites come back again
From grassy grave and urn.

From "All Saints' Eve" by Rose Terry Cooke (1827–92), published in the *Atlantic Monthly* in 1880. The poem goes on to plead for the spirit of a dear one to return; showing that the idea of loving souls making contact at Hallowe'en had not entirely disappeared by the end of the 19th century.

Souling

In the Middle Ages and later, Hallowmas was a time for charitable giving. The monks of Cluny Abbey distributed food to the poor on All Souls' Day, and the inhabitants of many towns and villages were called upon to remember the souls of the dead in their prayers. Poor folk, often children, would knock on doors, seeking food or money in return for offering up prayers for the householder's dead relatives. It became customary to bake bread or cakes especially for the occasion, and those doing the rounds in search of these "soul cakes" were referred to as going souling. "A soul cake. A soul cake. Have mercy on all Christian souls for a soul cake" is one of the traditional entreaties that survives. In time, singing, dancing, rhyming, and generally providing a little entertainment were all added to the more serious business of praying for departed souls.

Baking and sharing soul cakes dates back to at least the 15th century in England and parts of Europe, and the tradition continues in some places where Hallowe'en is celebrated. These days soul cakes can be anything from light, fluffy buns to flat, round cookies or biscuits. In the old days, there may also have been different versions, depending on location, but they were probably all made with spices, such as nutmeg, allspice, or cinnamon, as well as raisins and currants, and marked with a cross on top, to show they were alms. In Yorkshire, in the north of England, parkin—a kind of sticky gingerbread—is traditional on Bonfire Night, November 5, and may well have derived from soul cakes. If you want to bake soul cakes for Hallowe'en, you can find recipes galore online.

Soul, soul, for a souling cake,
I pray, good missus, a souling cake.
Apple or pear, a plum or a cherry,
Any good thing to make us all merry.

A medieval rhyme sung by children
going souling

21

GUISING

Before venturing out on All Hallows' Eve, whether to go souling or for some other purpose, people would often try to disguise themselves, allegedly to escape the notice of any stray wandering spirit. It could be the soul of someone they preferred not to meet and it was safer not to be recognized. At least, this may have been how it started. Some dressed up as saints to fool the spirits, some as supernatural beings, and in parts of Wales and Scotland, young people occasionally turned into gender benders, dressing as the opposite sex. Some merely put their clothes on inside out—although that doesn't seem much of a disguise. Maybe it was just a gesture to acknowledge the custom, or maybe it once had another significance, now forgotten. In some places, short costume plays, usually representing the triumph of good over evil, were performed from house to house in return for soul cakes or other food, or money.

However it was observed, Hallowmas was an event that nobody could ignore. All Saints' Day and All Souls' Day were both solemn days of holy obligation, and by then the notion of witchcraft was certainly real and feared, but nevertheless it's hard to avoid the idea that, serious occasion or not, it was also a great deal of fun.

When the practice of putting on a disguise to go out at Hallowmas faded away, or whether it carried on in some places, or was transferred to other times of year, such as Christmas, is not clear, but certainly in Scotland at the end of the 19th century "guising," as it was then called, was not unusual. Children disguised as supernatural beings, carrying carved-out turnips with candles inside, visited houses to be given cakes, nuts, apples, or money. But first they had to put on a show by reciting a poem, singing a song, or telling a joke. Hallowe'en guising continues in Scotland to this day, but the idea of performance and reward seems to have fallen by the wayside. Now it's more in line with American trick-or-treating.

When Queen Victoria visited her Scottish residence, Balmoral, one fall, Hallowe'en was marked with a huge bonfire and the burning of a hideous witch in effigy. The old witch, the Shandy Dann, was hauled into the grounds with much ceremony, accompanied by clansmen playing the bagpipes and an entourage of goblins, elves, and pixies, and was hurled into the flames while the onlookers cheered and the fairies melted away into the shadows. Much merry-making ensued and, for once, the queen was highly amused.

In some parts of Ireland, the guisers included a man draped in a white sheet and either wearing a horse's mask or carrying a decorated horse's skull on a pole. At each house the group would speak their verses and sing their songs and afterward were offered food in return for the "horse," the Muck Olla, bringing the householder good fortune for the coming year. In Wales, the "horse," which represented a gray mare, was known as the Mari Lwyd, and was often taken around at Christmas, rather than Hallowe'en.

An American holiday

Fall festivals have long been abundant all over America, varying from state to state and from county to county, so how did Hallowe'en come to be a nationwide holiday, celebrated with such enthusiasm by all ages, and second only to Christmas in terms of financial outlay?

It first came to prominence in the mid-19th century, when what had been a trickle of immigrants from Europe turned into a positive tsunami. Wave upon wave of Irish arrived in just a couple of years, escaping from starvation in their homeland. A combination of potato blight, failed harvests, high taxes, and no effective famine relief led to millions taking ship for the New World.

In Scotland, the Highland Clearances of the 18th and first part of the 19th centuries contributed to many Scots heading for Canada and America. An economy in dire straits, and landowners increasingly relying on sheep to get them out of trouble, led to mass evictions from the land. When this was coupled with financial inducements to emigrate, many of the poorest had no choice. As time went on, unemployment, and little prospect of finding jobs, led to many more, often skilled craftsmen, choosing to relocate to the land of opportunity in the hope and belief of finding a better life and building a future for their families.

Naturally, the new arrivals brought with them the customs and traditions of their birthplace, and among these was the keeping of October 31, All Hallows' Eve, with attendant festivities. To start with, this did not go down too well in New England, which remained a strictly Protestant region where Puritan values were upheld and folk didn't hold with such frivolities. In Maryland and places farther south, though, the event was welcomed. There, people got together for community celebrations, with singing and dancing, stories, and fortune telling—all rather low-key compared with today.

Once the Irish and Scots started arriving in numbers, however, not to mention other European and African immigrants, the idea of Hallowe'en spread rapidly. Americans discovered that this old festival could be fun, and embraced it with open arms.

balloon ghosts

No Hallowe'en party would be complete without a bunch of visiting ghosts, and these balloon spooks couldn't be easier to make. A piece of cheap cotton muslin is hung over a balloon with creepy features made from black card. Tie them in place to decorate a dull corner or fasten them by the front door to welcome trick-or-treaters to your home.

You will need

White balloon

White ribbon

59 in. (150 cm) square of white cotton muslin for each ghost

Scissors

Approximately 6 in. (15 cm) square of black card

Pencil

Glue

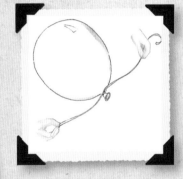

1 Blow the balloon up. Take a length of ribbon, making sure that it is long enough for the ghost to be hung up. Tie the ribbon securely around the balloon knot.

2 Fold the muslin in half and then into quarters. Make a small snip at the folded corner point using the scissors.

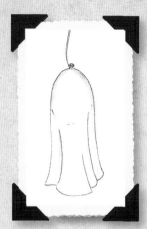

3 Unfold the muslin and thread the ribbon through the hole, pulling the muslin down over the balloon.

4 Draw two wobbly eyes and a wide, round mouth onto the black card. Cut them out neatly.

5 Stick the eyes and mouth onto the muslin over the balloon using the glue. Make sure they are well stuck down. Create a collection of ghosts, making the facial features different for each one. Hang the ghosts in place using the ribbon.

You wouldn't believe
On All Hallows' Eve
What lots of fun we can make,
With apples to bob
And nuts on the hob,
And a ring-and-thimble cake.

Carolyn Wells (1862–1942), author and poet

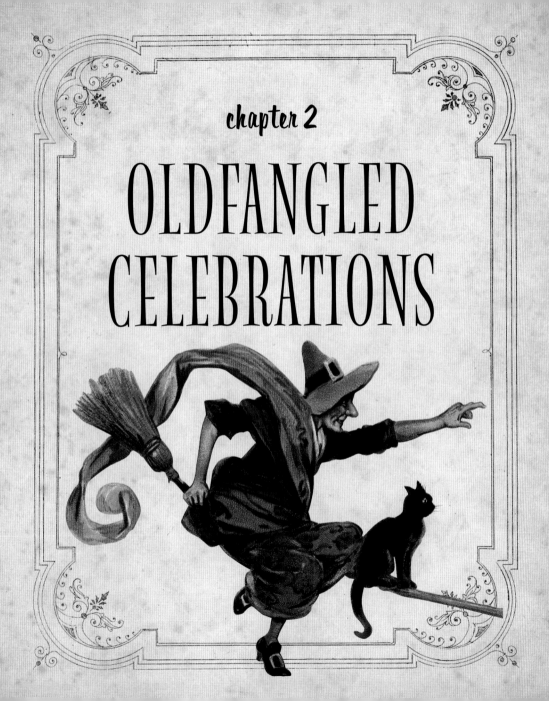

chapter 2

OLDFANGLED CELEBRATIONS

PARTIES

Romantic Victorian notions of recreating what
may have seemed a happier, more innocent past,
and gothic ideas of mystery and mysticism,
gradually gave way to the view that Hallowe'en
was actually a cheerful, frivolous occasion, the
scariness all pretend, the shivers down the spine
all pleasurable. Superstitions may have lingered
—people still crossed their fingers, just in case—
but it was fun to be spooked. And the kids loved it.

Celebration and revelry

According to Ruth Edna Kelley in *The Book of Hallowe'en*, published in 1919, "Hallowe'en parties are the real survival of ancient merrymakings." Glitzy balls, hotel getaways, wild all-night revelry, comfortable family get-togethers, children's parties—the whole spectrum of social gatherings marked Hallowe'en in the early 20th century, from the lavish to the homey. Although the occasion was generally geared toward children, adults happily joined in and created their own Hallowe'en-themed celebrations. The upper echelons of society, in particular, threw themselves into it with gusto, while Irish-American and Scottish-American societies, keen to keep the old traditions alive, continued to put on dinners and dances, often featuring renditions of Robert Burns' poem "Hallowe'en," written in 1785.

Ever since Irish and Scottish immigrants had started to arrive in large numbers, the entertainment at Hallowe'en parties had been mainly based on Robert Burns' imaginary tale of one Hallowe'en night in rural Scotland. The poem features customs long-established in those parts and, from the mid-19th century on, those traditions were willingly embraced by increasing numbers of Americans, probably without realizing the origins of the games and charms they were perpetuating with such enthusiasm.

After the games, everyone gathered round to tell one another ghost stories and other weird and wonderful tales. If this could be by the flickering light of a live flame, so much the better. No one (or not many people!) professed to believe in ghosts, witches, and fairies any more, but at such a time, and for anyone afraid of the dark, doubts may easily flood the mind…

It's a HALLOWEEN PARTY

"After the supper table has been cleared of all except the decorations and candles, have a large dish filled with burning alcohol and salt brought in and placed in the center. Seated around this ghostly fire, all other lights except the candles having been extinguished, let the guests tell stirring stories rigmarole fashion; that is, some one starting the story and stopping short at its most exciting point and letting his neighbor continue it, each one trying to make it as interesting as possible."

Mrs. Herbert B. Linscott, *Bright Ideas for Entertaining* (1905)

Ruth Edna Kelley has a variation on this:
"After all the charms have been tried, fagots [bunches of sticks and twigs bundled together] are passed about, and by the eerie light of burning salt and alcohol, ghost stories are told, each concluding his installment as his fagot withers to ashes. Sometimes cabbage stalks used in the omens take the place of fagots."

Ruth Edna Kelley, *The Book of Hallowe'en* (1919)

For parties held in private houses, secrecy ruled. No one told anyone else they were invited and guests came disguised, wearing masks and dressed up as ghosts, witches, goblins, or anything else deemed appropriate. "All formality must be dispensed with on Hallowe'en," according to Mrs. Linscott in her *Bright Ideas for Entertaining* (1905). "Not only will quaint customs and mystic tricks be in order, but the decorations and refreshments, and even the place of meeting, must be as strange and mystifying as possible." Mrs. L suggests a "roomy barn" as ideal, or a "large attic, running the entire length of

the house," but if the "ambitious hostess" is not fortunate enough to have either of these at her disposal, the kitchen has to be the "place of meeting and mystery," with party refreshments laid out in the suitably decorated dining room.

"The decorations need not be expensive to be charming"—a key point when preparing a vintage Hallowe'en celebration. "Large vases of ferns and chrysanthemums and umbrella stands of fluffy grasses will be desirable; but if these cannot be readily obtained, quantities of gayly tinted autumn leaves will be quite appropriate. Festoons of nuts, bunches of wheat or oats, and strings of cranberries may also help to brighten the wall decorations, and the nuts and cranberries will be useful in many odd arrangements for ornamenting the refreshment table." It's clear that Mrs. Linscott is following the harvest-party tradition with her décor, although she does suggest that the room is lit with candles and Jack o' lanterns—no mention of fire risk, so perhaps a degree of common sense was assumed in those days—and the earlier mention of "mystic tricks" is intriguing. She does advocate playing fortune-telling games and the telling of ghostly tales, so perhaps that's what she meant. Ruth Edna Kelley suggests harvest decorations, too, and adds "a frieze of witches on broomsticks, with

The idea of a fall party, brightening up what could be a dull time of year, was certainly not new. Before the masses of immigrants arrived, harvest "play parties" took place in many regions of America. First came the work of preserving and storing the year's produce, followed by music, dancing, fortune-telling games, eating, drinking, and generally making merry.

34

cats, bats, and owls," and "ghosts and skulls and cross-bones, symbols of death, [to] startle the beholder."

When the idea of parades took hold, around the 1930s, community gatherings in civic centers, classrooms, or halls became fashionable, although home parties were still popular. "Everyone loves a ghost party," says Ida Baily Allen in *When You Entertain: What To Do, And How* (1932). "… Instruct the guests to come in ghostly garb. Have the room darkened, and as they enter the guests should be greeted with a ghostly handclasp; a wet glove filled with sand gives the desired effect." Now there's an idea for your vintage Hallowe'en party!

Postwar, Hallowe'en parties were mostly for children. Once those kids grew up, though, they didn't want to miss out on the fun, and so from around the 1980s, more and more adults were joining in, dressing up to supervise their kids' trick-or-treating and partying afterward in bars, restaurants, or other designated venues, or even at home.

From Your
SECRET PAL!
(guess who says Boo!)

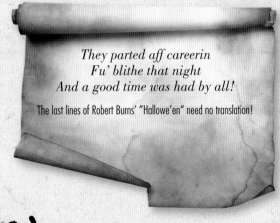

*They parted aff careerin
Fu' blithe that night
And a good time was had by all!*

The last lines of Robert Burns' "Hallowe'en" need no translation!

PRANKS

Once the idea of a Hallowe'en holiday had taken hold, it became a great excuse for pranks and mischief. Youths and young men let off steam with a series of jolly japes. The college students of Lafayette, Pennsylvania, had a great time in 1887, as reported in the *New York Times*. "This morning the chapel bell sounded very faintly, which was not strange considering that a hammer served in place of the clapper, which was mysteriously missing." Stepladders from the college and hymn books from the chapel were deposited in a hole dug in the grounds. The students hid dumbbells and the tennis net, and filled the keyholes of the chapel doors with molten lead. Best of all, "The college horse spent the night on the first floor of McKeen Hall." There's no mention of how they got the old nag up there, or down again the next morning, or of the cleaning-up operation.

Inevitably, though, some of the japes became less jolly, and in 1912 the recently formed Boy Scouts got together with various boys' clubs and other organizations to call for safe Hallowe'en celebrations. Posters in schools promoted a "Sane Hallowe'en," but mischief-making was all part of it and the pranks went on to the enormous entertainment of many people, especially the perpetrators, and the annoyance of many others. In Alberta in 1927, one newspaper reported: "Hallowe'en provided an opportunity for real strenuous fun. No real damage was done except to the temper of some who had to hunt for wagon wheels, gates, wagons, barrels, etc., much of which decorated the front street."

Gates were particularly vulnerable, for some reason. Much fun was to be had in

A joke that misfired

The Capitol, no less, was the scene of one prank that went wrong. A police officer, who had recently started in the job, was on duty on the night of October 31, 1885. All was in darkness as he made a routine patrol, which was uneventful until he came to the Statuary Hall where he heard the sound of groaning coming from one corner of the room. Approaching warily, the officer saw, or thought he saw, a spectral figure. What else to do but shoot it? So he drew his gun and fired, several times. Fortunately, he missed. The "spectral figure" turned out to be a fellow officer playing a Hallowe'en prank on the new boy. This story has entered the annals of Capitol history, but what happened to the two officers concerned does not appear to be recorded.

detaching them and leaving them somewhere unlikely, on shed roofs for instance, and swapping gates was clearly hysterically funny, so much so that in various states, Hallowe'en became known as Gate Night.

Householders would answer a knock on the door to find no one there (ghost rapping), door bells were jammed on, and door knockers stolen or covered in candle grease. Soaping windows was a great favorite, and throwing eggs at windows and doors another. Wagons and buggies and anything else movable ended up in a pile in the street, or in someone else's front yard, or on a roof somewhere. And pranksters were drawn to outhouses like iron filings to a magnet. Pushing over an outside privy was just irresistible, and if it happened to be occupied at the time, that was like hitting the jackpot.

The boys—and some girls—played the usual Hallowe'en tricks on Tuesday night, carrying away gates, overturning outhouses and raising a merry disturbance all around. The sufferers from these pranks took it as a matter of course, and quietly hunted up their property again on Wednesday.

Carbon County Journal, 1899. Girls were not going to be left out in Wyoming—then or later. In 1911, the *Rawlins Republican* reported that "'thirty or forty young ladies' almost succeeded in tying a police officer who accosted them to a telephone pole with a rope" (rawlinstimes.com). Not a good idea to try that today!

Hallowe'en parties were one way of keeping potential mischief-makers off the streets. "Boys will be far less apt to carry off the clothes-posts, unhinge the gates and make night hideous if you give them a part in keeping with the occasion—a party [with] tin horns…where paper caps adorn the head and where jack-lanterns adorn the room…" Annie Gregory's suggestion in 1901

(from *The Blue Ribbon Cook Book*)

It's HALLOWEEN!

Bring turnips scoop'd, and bladders blown;
Bring the sling, and bring the stone,
This for window, that for door;
Instruments a thousand more,
Thou shalt bring for urchin-play,
On the truant holyday!

From "*An Ode to Fun*," Rev. George Butt 1789

"Bladders blown" may refer to the practice of inflating a pig's bladder to make a ball. Or could it be that children in those days filled the bladder with water and then let it go to whizz around at random and drench anyone unlucky enough to be nearby—much as later generations did (and perhaps still do) with balloons? But slinging stones at windows? Perhaps he meant ones without glass in them!

Mischief Night

In some places this became another name for Hallowe'en, in others it was observed on the night before. Its origins are obscure. It probably came from England, specifically Yorkshire, although in 1790, in a record of proceedings at Oxford University, which is some way south of Yorkshire, mention is made of "An Ode to Fun which praises children's tricks on Mischief Night in most approving terms." In those days, Mischief Night was a rural affair, which took place on the eve of May Day, April 30, but with the coming of the Industrial Revolution and the mass movement of people from country to town, the date shifted to November 4, the eve of Bonfire Night and the ceremonial burning of an effigy of Guy Fawkes—one of a group of conspirators who made an unsuccessful attempt to blow up king and parliament in 1605.

Once the Industrial Revolution got under way, folk from Yorkshire began to emigrate to North America in numbers. Craftsmen and their families, who had been put out of work by mechanization, tended to settle together in groups, including in Pennsylvania and Rhode Island. Of course, they brought their Mischief Night traditions with them, and somehow these merged with the Hallowe'en customs brought by the Irish and Scots.

Other names for Mischief Night are Prank Night, Beggars' Night (possibly linking it to early forms of trick-or-treating), and Goosey Night. Soaping windows, chalking screen doors, egg bombing, toilet-papering yards, ringing doorbells and running away—all the usual Hallowe'en pranks were to be expected. In the midwest, the event was known as Corn Night, because corn husks were the missile of choice to throw on front porches and at windows. In the northeast it was cabbages, so Mischief Night became known as Cabbage Night.

41

Among the mischief-making, some of the more complicated pranks seem to have involved hard work, not to mention a fair amount of courage. Around 1890, in Grand Junction, Colorado, one group of determined young boys dismantled a heavy wagon, took it 80 ft (24 m) (!) up a ladder to the top of a steel water tower, and reassembled it there for all to see. The next day, the bemused owner paid some likely-looking lads, who just happened to be hanging around, to go up and bring it down again—same boys, so all that effort paid off in the end!

Dismantling wagons and reassembling them in the least likely places seems to have been a favorite exercise. Perhaps it was a case of once one gang had done it, everyone else wanted to have a go—although an 80 ft water tower would take some beating. Shorty Burch of Tucson reminisced in the *Tucson Examiner*: "Bud and I took old man Johnson's buggy apart piece by piece. Then we climbed up on a roof and reassembled it. Of course, everyone knew it was us, and Dad made us take it down and put it together the next day." No reward for Shorty, then, except the

satisfaction of having done it!

However, there's a fine line to be drawn between the "strenuous fun" reported in Alberta and vandalism, and as time went on, that line was crossed more and more often. Damaging property, turning on fire hydrants, setting wagons ablaze, letting livestock out— at Anoka in Minnesota, cows were found wandering down Main Street—were all going too far. Something had to be done.

"This is Orson Welles, ladies and gentlemen, out of character to assure you that 'The War of the Worlds' has no further significance than as the holiday offering it was intended to be. The Mercury Theater's own radio version of dressing up in a sheet and jumping out of a bush and saying 'Boo!' Starting now, we couldn't soap all your windows and steal all your garden gates by tomorrow night... so we did the next best thing. We annihilated the world before your very ears... You will be relieved, I hope, to learn that we didn't mean it... That grinning, glowing, globular invader of your living room is an inhabitant of the pumpkin patch, and if your doorbell rings and nobody's there, that was no Martian, it's Halloween."

A radio drama based on H.G. Wells' book *The War of the Worlds*, published in 1898, had caused widespread panic. Many people believed it was a live news broadcast and the country really was under alien attack. Afterward, its star, Orson Welles, explained the reasoning behind the production. The date was October 30, 1938.

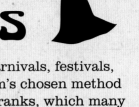

Parades

It seems that civic celebrations, such as carnivals, festivals, street parties, and parades, were officialdom's chosen method of discouraging the playing of Hallowe'en pranks, which many youngsters had taken to so enthusiastically as to make them downright antisocial. If that was the case, the plan worked and vandalism was curtailed when entertainment was laid on.

Anoka in Minnesota was one of the first places to host a citywide celebration. In 1920, local bands and various clubs and other organizations marched through town together with representatives of the police, National Guard, and fire service, and hundreds of children. Afterward, all the children who had taken part were given candy, nuts, and popcorn, and everyone went to an enormous bonfire party. The event was such a success that it was decided to carry on with it, and pretty soon there were two parades, one during the day and one in the evening. Other entertainment included the Pumpkin Bowl (a football game), window-painting and house-decorating competitions, pillow fights, costume contests, concerts, story-telling, races, and fireworks. The Anoka parade has been staged every year since 1920, with the exception of the war years, 1942 and 1943.

It wasn't long before other cities followed suit. Allentown, Pennsylvania, had apparently been having smaller Hallowe'en parades from 1905 but upped its game in the 1920s. New York City staged a Hallowe'en carnival in 1923, and from 1936 Central Park Mall, Manhattan, was the party venue. In 1939, a parade in Newark, New Jersey, drew a crowd of 300,000. The idea spread, and all over America, October 31 became official party time! Today, New York City's annual Village Hallowe'en Parade attracts thousands upon thousands of participants and spectators. Tall rod puppets are skillfully manipulated by puppeteers, and elaborate floats carry live bands. The costumed, face-painted, and masked—anyone can join in, the more flamboyant the better.

These days, Anaheim in California is synonymous with Disneyland, but in the early 1920s it was a quiet farming town, the residents of which were increasingly fed up with Hallowe'en pranks that were getting out of hand. Soaped windows were one thing, damaged property another. So in 1923, in order to divert these disruptive tendencies, the town held an official Hallowe'en party with games and costume contests. Problem solved! In 1924 the festival included a night parade—the procession led by baseball superstars Babe Ruth and Walter Johnson—and every year since then, witches, ghosts, fairies, and all else beside have floated through the streets of Anaheim to great acclaim. Walt Disney sponsored the parade in 1953—probably thanking his lucky stars for such a heaven-sent promotional opportunity.

Disneyland opened its gates in 1955, and the Hallowe'en festival went from strength to strength.

Hallowe'en capital

Anoka is the self-proclaimed Hallowe'en capital of the world, but it has a competitor. Salem in Massachusetts claims the same title—ironic, really, in the light of Salem's history, but of course the story of the witch trials attracts a lot of tourists to the town, especially at Hallowe'en.

Haunted Attractions
and Midnight Horror Shows

"Let's go to a haunting" is a common cry at the end of October, but the history of Hallowe'en haunted attractions is hard to discover. Commercial haunted houses, experiences, forest trails, corn mazes, hayrides, and screamparks seem to have come on the scene from around the 1970s and are now sophisticated, highly technical operations. To start with, some may have been used for fundraising—you paid to be scared, a bit like a dark ride or ghost train at a fun fair.

However, for the dedicated Hallowe'en party-giver in the 1930s and 1940s, haunted rooms seem to have been the latest thing. Darkly decked out with fanciful and spooky trimmings and flourishes, the party room was the venue for games and subterfuges designed either to thrill or scare the kids rigid—encouraging a blindfolded child to poke a finger into a soft orange and then telling him it was an eye, for example. Apparently, the stunts and tricks became more elaborate with each year, but the children, and their parents, must have known more or less what to expect. Those of a nervous disposition were probably confined to knocking on welcoming neighbors' doors to rattle their trick-or-treat buckets.

46

Around the same time, theaters were offering live shows by magicians and mind-readers, using ghostly special effects to amaze audiences. At Hallowe'en these shows were often followed by horror movies, a recently established film genre at the time. Watching these black-and-white movies, usually adapted from Victorian gothic novels, became a popular feature

Horror movies

Any one of these would add an especially scary note to your vintage Hallowe'en festivities, but if possible make sure the movie is a black-and-white original.

Dr Jekyll and Mr Hyde, *1920*	The Old Dark House, *1932*
Nosferatu, *1922*	The Ghoul, *1933*
The Phantom of the Opera, *1925*	The Black Cat, *1934*
Dracula, *1931*	The Raven, *1935*
Frankenstein, *1931*	Bride of Frankenstein, *1935*
The Mummy, *1932*	The Creature from the Black Lagoon, *1954*

Harry Houdini

The famous escapologist, magician, and stuntman was also a keen debunker of fraudsters. He made it his business to expose fake psychics, spiritualists, mediums, and anyone who was likely to give his profession a bad name. In his time, he escaped from chains, shackles, handcuffs, and straitjackets, often while nailed in packing cases or tied in mailbags and dumped under water. In one stunt, he was buried alive. He was a master of his craft and his name is still synonymous with seemingly impossible escapes. Houdini died of peritonitis in 1926, on Hallowe'en.

of Hallowe'en. As time went on and the special effects, both live and on screen, became more gory, the shows were put on later in the evening and became known as midnight horror shows. By the 1960s, the public's enthusiasm for them had faded and they were abandoned, but the idea of watching horror movies at Hallowe'en has never gone out of style.

haunted house lanterns

Add to Hallowe'en's spooky theme with a haunted house, lit from inside to create an eerie glow. Even better, why not have a row of them? You can put them on a side table, mantelpiece, or window sill—wherever a little extra creepiness is required. Make your houses from gray cardboard, and in two sizes, adding wonky windows and wooden bars to make them look suitably rickety. Use battery-operated votives (tea lights) inside the lanterns, and keep them well away from lit candles.

You will need

Templates on pages 138–39

Pencil

Scissors

16 x 10 in. (40 x 26 cm) gray cardboard for each house

Craft knife and cutting mat

Metal ruler

8in. (20cm) square thin black card for each house

Glue stick

Orange tissue paper

Wooden popsicle (lollipop) sticks

Rotary hole punch

Battery-operated votives (tea lights)

1 Use the templates on pages 138–39 to draw the basic shapes for the front and back of the house and cut them out from gray cardboard, cutting out the spaces for windows and door where indicated. Use the craft knife and cutting mat to make clean, neat cuts, using a metal ruler, if you find it helpful. Do the same for the smaller house, if you're making that, too.

2 Use the templates on page 138 to cut out windows and door from black card.

3 Glue the black windows and door over the holes allowed for them, pressing them down to make sure they are well stuck.

4 Cut a piece of orange tissue paper 4 x 4½ in. (10 x 11.5 cm) and glue onto the back of the windows and door. For the smaller house, cut a piece that is 4 x 4 in. (10 x 10 cm).

5 Use the craft knife and cutting mat to score along the fold lines on the inside of the house, making sure that you do not cut into the card too much. Fold along the score lines and apply glue along the flap you have created. Stick the house together.

6 Cut short strips of black card (from the templates on page 139) and glue them to the front of the house to create a rickety fence. Cut two pieces of popsicle (lollipop) stick about 1½ in. (4 cm) long and glue them across a window or a door. Draw tiny nails onto both ends of the popsicle sticks. Cut out bats and spiders from black card (from the templates on page 139) and glue them onto the front of the house.

7 Cut out a roof (from the templates on pages 138–39), choosing to leave it plain or to cut a scalloped or jagged edge. Punch holes along the scalloped edge with the hole punch. If you're making three houses, you could have one of each roof type.

8 Score the edge of the roof along the fold lines using the craft knife, and fold along the score lines.

9 Cut out a chimney (from the template on page 139), fold along the line, and glue it onto the roof. Place the battery-operated votive (tea light) inside the house and put the roof on top.

cobweb tablecloth

An appropriately decorated party table really does help to create the right atmosphere, and the best place to start is with the table covering. Inexpensive cotton muslin can be turned into a delightfully cobwebby feature, which will grab all the attention if draped over another cloth of solid black. Older children may like to help—since when did they get praise instead of being told off for tearing something?! Perhaps younger children can help to collect ivy twigs—scattered round and about, the greenery adds to the ambience of an old-fashioned Hallowe'en.

You will need

Large piece of black fabric, enough to cover your table and hang down to reach the floor

Length of cotton muslin, enough to cover your table and hang more than halfway down the sides

Sharp fabric scissors

1 Lay the black fabric on the table. Cut away the selvage from both edges of the muslin. Place it over the top of the black fabric so that it reaches about halfway down the table. Cut a small snip in the edge of the muslin.

2 Take hold of the muslin either side of the snip you have just made and pull to tear the muslin.

3 Make a cut into the tear at an angle and pull the threads along the cut edge to make it look more ragged.

4 Now make a hole in the muslin, again with the scissors, cutting it roughly.

5 Tear the muslin around the hole, making the edges look rough. Continue to cut and tear the muslin all the way round randomly from the bottom up, and make holes wherever you feel they're needed.

Front-porch and yard decorations

Elaborate animatronic displays, Hallowe'en inflatables, and all the many sophisticated yard decorations available today are of relatively recent origin. In fact, before the 1990s, most Hallowe'en yard decorations were homemade. At one time, most if not all decorations were put up inside the house rather than outside, especially for parties or dinners.

The idea of adorning the porch and yard more or less coincided with the advent of trick-or-treating. Probably, once one or two people in the neighborhood made the effort, others would have followed suit.

Jack o' lanterns were already universal and had been the main Hallowe'en decoration for many years. After that, it depended whether you wanted to celebrate the harvest aspect of Hallowe'en with scarecrows, corn shocks, and piles of nuts and apples, or venture down the scary path with silhouettes of witches, black cats, spiders, and bats—or mix the two.

Scarecrows

These symbols of the harvest have been adopted into the Hallowe'en family. Scarecrows are protectors, and a scarecrow in the yard guards the house. They have a long history, dating back to ancient Greece, Rome, and Japan, although probably not in their familiar modern form.

Years ago, Native Americans had bird scarers. In Virginia and the Carolinas, adults sat on raised wooden platforms and yelled their heads off when birds landed in the corn. The colonists patrolled their fields to scare off birds with shouts, arm-waving, and stones, as they had in their homelands. The Pilgrims used to bury fish in the cornfields as fertilizer and so had the added task of chasing away other hungry creatures attracted by the smell, as well as birds.

By the late 1800s, the idea of non-human bird scarers must have taken hold, because children of the southwest tribes were having competitions to see who could make the most unusual and frightening scarecrow. The one brought by German immigrants to Pennsylvania, a bootzamon or boogeyman, seems to be the most recognizable—a wooden cross shape draped with overalls and other old clothes, a mop top for a head or a roundish bundle of cloth stuffed with straw, with an old straw hat. A vintage scarecrow would look similar to that, maybe with a pumpkin for a head, and over the years has remained remarkably unchanged. Scarecrows were common up until the Second World War, when sprays took over the job they were designed to do, so now they are rarely seen except at Hallowe'en when they appear in great numbers on front porches and in yards all over the country.

Vintage Spookiness

Choosing the theme and displaying the elements of your yard decorations are all part of the fun of Hallowe'en. To achieve a vintage look, the best advice is to keep it simple. Here are some suggestions for how to create some old-style mystery.

✽ Jack o' lanterns are obligatory, whether you have just one, a few, or many. Have them on the porch, lighting the front window of a darkened room, along the path, anywhere and everywhere!

✽ Festoon your front door, or trees in the yard, with fake mist, gauzy cobwebs, or shrouds, and have some cut-out bats, owls, black cats, witches, and spiders, and a skull or two. There are some templates at the back of the book to get you started.

Boo!

It's hard to discover just how this tradition originated, but Boo! cards do seem to exist from quite early last century. These days, the idea is to leave a small gift with a card, poem, or sign on two neighbors' doorsteps, anonymously. They leave the sign there and do the same for two more neighbors, and so on, until the whole area has been boo-ed. That's it! Perhaps that's the way it always was—it's nice to think so.

✱ Thickly coat a gourd or squash with white paint and let it dry. Then, with a thinner brush and black paint, or a black felt-tipped pen, add eyes, nose, and mouth—teeth, too, if you like. Make the face as scary or friendly as you wish. Several of these strategically placed around the porch should help the ambience.

✱ Make a large, imaginatively painted "Beware" sign to prop up where it will be easily seen—by the gate or mailbox, or by the front door, or in a tree. Find some wood, maybe an old shelf, or some spare MDF, or even thick card—signs can be upright or horizontal—and paint over it haphazardly in gray, black, or orange. Look up some vintage postcards and, in the same style, paint your board in a contrasting color with a message, such as "Enter at Your Own Risk," "Your Fate is in Your Own Hands," "Look Out! Look Out! Goblins About!," or you could choose welcoming words, such as "Knock for Candy" or just "Happy Hallowe'en."

✱ The odd headstone often fits in well, beside the path, under a tree, or by a bush. If making one seems too daunting, or if you're out of time or energy, foam ones are available to buy.

✱ Inside the house, you could arrange white sheets to look like ghosts in barely lit windows to fool trick-or-treaters.

✱ Maybe have a black-and-white horror movie playing at a darkened window so it can be seen from outside. See page 47 for suggestions.

✱ Strings of colored lights, orange, purple, and white, may not be strictly vintage, but they do add to the atmosphere.

JACK O' LANTERNS

According to popular belief, Hallowe'en Jack o' lanterns originated in Ireland, hundreds of years ago. They were also made in Scotland and England. Turnips, rutabagas (swedes), and sugar beets were hollowed out and carved with grotesque faces. An ember or candle placed inside made them even more startling. Beside keeping supernatural forces at bay, a Jack o' lantern was supposed to guide the souls of dead relatives back to their earthly abodes for just that one night. Later, irreverent youngsters would carve out and illuminate their turnips and leave them in lonely, shadowy places along the road to frighten the life out of anyone who happened to pass that way.

Legend of Stingy Jack

Many versions of this old Irish folktale exist, all telling more or less the same story of how the Jack o' lantern got its name.

Jack, a greedy, bad-tempered, parsimonious man, known as a liar, a cheat, and a trickster, unsurprisingly had few friends, but he enjoyed a drink. On his way home one night, he is accosted by the Devil. Fearing his time has come, Jack makes a final request—one more drink of ale. The Devil agrees and accompanies Jack to the nearest tavern to partake of a glass or two. When Jack asks the Devil to pay as agreed, the Devil, the greatest shapeshifter of them all, turns himself into a silver coin. Jack, not quite so befuddled as may be imagined, rather than paying for the ale, puts the coin in his pocket, where he carries a crucifix. The Devil is trapped. Once outside the alehouse, Jack offers a deal. He will set the Devil free in exchange for the Evil One leaving him alone for ten years. Ten years later, the Devil confronts Jack again. This time, Jack asks for an apple as his last request and the Devil, who seems a tad foolish in this tale, climbs a nearby tree to pick one. Jack, of course, quickly carves a few crosses in the bark, trapping the Devil again. Now the price of Jack's help is that the Devil should never claim his soul, and the fateful bargain is struck.

Jack, secure in the knowledge that he's never going to hell, carries on with his life as before, not worrying about the consequences. Unfortunately for him, when he eventually dies, he discovers there is no place for such a sinner in heaven and is unceremoniously turned away. He has no choice but to drag himself off to hell, where the Devil is adamant about keeping his promise made all those years ago. As Jack turns away, the Devil throws him a piece of burning coal and Jack, doomed to wander forever in search of a place to rest, hollows out a turnip and puts the coal inside to light him on his way. He always carries his light, and so becomes Jack of the lantern, which is shortened to Jack o' lantern.

Will o' the wisps

In folklore, Jack o' lanterns and Will o' the wisps, also known as spook-lights, ghost-lights, and ignis fatuus (*Latin for "foolish fire"*), are often interchangeable. Will o' the wisps were mysterious lights that appeared in lonely places at night to guide travelers, often away from the path and into dangerous territory, such as bogs, marshes, or swamps.

These eerie lights were known by various names around Britain and Europe, and many ghostly tales were attached to them. One story, very similar to the legend of Stingy Jack, has it that when Will the Smith, a bad-living blacksmith, died, he was given a second chance by St. Peter and sent back to Earth to have another go. He messed that one up, too, continuing his wicked ways, and so was condemned to wander for ever, a single burning ember his only light and comfort, with which he lures unsuspecting travelers into danger. Some people never change!

In fact, these treacherous and unearthly lights are thought to be caused by the spontaneous combustion of marsh gases, mostly methane, generated by rotting organic matter.

Pumpkin Carving

In America, pumpkin carving had long been associated with the harvest and Thanksgiving. So, when the idea of Hallowe'en really took hold with the arrival of huge numbers of Irish and Scottish immigrants in the 19th century, it was natural for the pumpkin to supersede the turnip in the Jack o' lantern stakes. They were easier to carve than any other vegetable, the tradition already existed, and, being native to America, they were readily available.

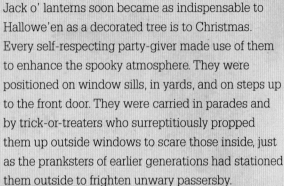

Jack o' lanterns soon became as indispensable to Hallowe'en as a decorated tree is to Christmas. Every self-respecting party-giver made use of them to enhance the spooky atmosphere. They were positioned on window sills, in yards, and on steps up to the front door. They were carried in parades and by trick-or-treaters who surreptitiously propped them up outside windows to scare those inside, just as the pranksters of earlier generations had stationed them outside to frighten unwary passersby.

These days they are often used by householders to indicate whether trick-or-treaters are welcome—a Jack o' lantern in the front yard or window means candy awaits. A pumpkin with a thinner skin than others, the Howden, is grown especially for carving. Making Jack o' lanterns at Hallowe'en is all part of the fun. See page 66–67 for instructions.

Jack o' the lantern! Joan the wad,
Who tickled the maid and
made her mad
Light me home the weather's bad.

Old rhyme from Cornwall, England, where the local name for a Jack o' lantern was Joan the Wad.

64

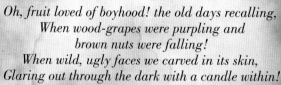

Oh, fruit loved of boyhood! the old days recalling,
When wood-grapes were purpling and
brown nuts were falling!
When wild, ugly faces we carved in its skin,
Glaring out through the dark with a candle within!

From "The Pumpkin" by John Greenleaf Whittier (1807–92)

A MERRY HALLOWE'EN

Pumpkin fests

These days pumpkin festivals (or pumpkin fests, or P-fests) are held in the run-up to Hallowe'en all over America. Amid the fun and games, the main aim is to see how many Jack o' lanterns can be lit at the same time. Keene in New Hampshire holds the world record (as recorded in the Guinness Book of Records), set on October 19, 2013, with 30,581.

grinning jack o' lantern

Where would a vintage Hallowe'en be without a glowing Jack o' lantern? You can't have one without the other! This traditional, scarily grinning face will have all your guests and callers shaking in their shoes with its eerie presence. Use either a special pumpkin-carving tool (available from craft stores and online companies) or a thin-bladed knife to work slowly and carefully around the curved lines. Never leave a lit candle or votive (tea light) unattended, and remove the lid if it starts to burn.

1 Draw a jagged line around the top of the pumpkin, making it the same distance from the stalk all the way around.

2 Carefully cut along all the jagged lines and gently ease off the lid.

You will need
Pencil
Pumpkin
Thin-bladed knife
Small, strong spoon
Template on page 137
Scrap paper
Scissors
Votive (tea light)

3 Scoop out the seeds and scrape out the interior with a spoon so that the flesh is about ¾ in. (2 cm) thick. Make sure you do not puncture the skin.

4 Using the template on page 137, cut out the features for the face from some scrap paper. Hold them in place on the pumpkin, piece by piece, and draw around them.

5 Cut through the curved pencil lines slowly and neatly, removing and discarding the cut-out pieces of pumpkin.

6 Cut vertical slits around the back of the pumpkin to let more light shine through. Make sure that slits are not too near the bottom of the pumpkin.

7 Put a votive (tea light) inside the pumpkin and light it with a taper or a long match. Then replace the lid, position the Jack o' lantern, and await reactions.

Trick-or-Treat

The origins of trick-or-treating are by no means clear cut, but in the form it takes now, it is almost certainly an American invention. The idea of it linking back to the old European traditions of souling and guising (see pages 21–23) is unproven, and possibly a tad fanciful, but no less beguiling for that.

Localized instances of children asking for gifts can be unearthed all around America. In Cleveland, Ohio, for instance, around the time of the First World War, "Masked children began to show up on doorsteps, chiming 'we want a handout'… costumed beggars were treated with cookies, popcorn balls, candy, doughnuts, and cider" (clevelandhistorical.org). From the 1920s, references to the term "trick-or-treat" appear sporadically in various local newspapers—one of the first in Alberta in 1927: "The youthful tormentors were at back door and front demanding edible plunder by the word 'trick-or-treat' to which the inmates gladly responded and sent the robbers away rejoicing." In just a few decades, the rules of this new game plan seem to have spread by osmosis right across America, hindered temporarily by sugar rationing from 1942 to 1947. Children are not slow to catch on to a trend

Trick-or-Treat for UNICEF

In 1950, Reverend Clyde Allison and his wife, Mary Emma, had a bright idea. Why not encourage kids to collect money for disadvantaged children, rather than candy for themselves? So that year a group of youngsters in Philadelphia collected a total of $17 in decorated milk cartons and sent it to UNICEF. That's how the campaign Trick-or-Treat for UNICEF started. With official backing, the milk cartons were replaced by small orange collection boxes, the scheme became a nationwide campaign, and the total now stands at more than $170 million and rising.

that's both fun and mischievous, and while one theory suggests that adults introduced the game of trick-or-treat (as a form of bribery to deter pranksters), it seems more likely to have been the other way around, and children developed it for themselves.

If how it started is a matter of some debate, there is no doubt that it was not universally acclaimed. Some adults thought it smacked of extortion—and in some places, if the trick-or-treaters were teenagers, it may well have seemed threatening. Some people thought it was just ritualized begging, and others that it merely encouraged children to embrace consumerism.

On HALLOWEEN You Better Watch Out!

It has to be said that children didn't need much encouragement in that direction if what was on offer was both desirable and delicious. In the fullness of time, national children's magazines, such as *Jack and Jill*, and popular radio programs, including "The Jack Benny Show" and "The Adventures of Ozzie and Harriet," cottoned on to the practice's increasing popularity, and by the 1950s, it had really come into its own—it was even the subject of a Donald Duck cartoon, "Trick or Treat," in 1952. Thus given credibility, and official UNICEF backing in 1953, it went on to become the main focus of Hallowe'en, which has turned into a happy occasion when grown-ups and kids get to dress up and go out to play together.

A reference to what may have been an early form of trick-or-treating appeared in 1911 in a newspaper in Kingston, Ontario. A report mentioned that, as usual, children were rewarded with nuts and candy for singing and reciting poems as they progressed around stores and neighbors between 6 and 7 p.m. However, such an event was by no means usual elsewhere, and none of the postcards that were so popular in the early 20th century depicted, or referred to, trick-or-treating—at least, none that have so far come to light.

CANDY

Hallowe'en and candy came together in a big way in the 1950s. Candy was an easy treat to hand out to the increasing numbers of young callers. Whichever came first, supply or demand, it was a happy partnership, and by the 1970s, candy was really the only treat expected or given.

Before that, it was just one of several things given out, including fruit, especially candy (toffee) apples, nuts, and even coins. By the 1920s, a few manufacturers had decided that Hallowe'en could be a marketing opportunity, but no greater than any other holiday time, such as Christmas. Gumdrops and jelly beans, among other candies, were made in black and orange, and packaging was designed to match: "…Hallowe'en candy boxes—witch and black cat decorations on them—and ultimately tied with wonderful pompons of black…ribbon." (This is from "Hallowe'en Fal-Lalls and Fare," an article by Jane Edington published in the *Chicago Daily Tribune*, October 23, 1921.) But such beautifully wrapped offerings seem to be more for giving as gifts at parties than to thrust into the outstretched hands of young trick-or-treaters, who would be more likely to appreciate the contents than the tasteful trimmings.

Trick-or-treating candy was virtually all homemade, or at least handed over as individual offerings, up until the 1960s and 1970s, when a series of particularly nasty rumors swept the land, involving handouts being laced with poison and razor blades. Despite these stories being untrue, parents became understandably cautious about what their children could accept, and since then Hallowe'en candy has tended to be shop-bought and wrapped so as to be tamper-free.

So, strictly speaking, candy has no special part to play in vintage Hallowe'en, but since that idea may not go down too well with the younger generation, why not indulge in some retro candy? Candy corn, also known as "chicken feed," was first made in the 1880s, and a hundred or so years ago, it's not inconceivable that children would have enjoyed it as a sweet treat at holiday time. Hershey chocolate bars and Brach's candy are other possibilities, and for a party, candy (toffee) apples and popcorn balls are a must.

HALLOWE'EN FARE

Certain foods are forever associated with Hallowe'en, even if they are not all for eating—pumpkins, apples, and nuts, for instance, the last two essential for games and for fortune-telling as much as for munching. "Plain, hearty fare" was called for, which included gingerbread, doughnuts, and popcorn, as well as various savories, salads, and sandwiches, preferably made with homemade bread.

"Arrange huge platters of gingerbread at each corner, with dishes of plain candies and nuts here and there, and pyramids of fruit that will be quickly demolished when the guests are grouped about the table."

Mrs. Herbert B. Linscott, *Bright Ideas for Entertaining* (1905).
They were healthy eaters in those days if the fruit was so popular.

Much vintage Hallowe'en fare has one thing in common—hidden-charm syndrome. In many instances, the food was an extension of the fortune-telling and divination games imported from the Old World and embraced so wholeheartedly by the New. Symbolic talismans found their way into all sorts of different dishes, and the custom is still followed today, enthusiasm for it undimmed by passing time or any supposed increase in sophistication. Perhaps it's nostalgia for pursuing the old ways—or perhaps it's still just fun!

"When you think of Hallowe'en you generally think of cider, too. But you can moderate that standard drink by serving it hot and spiced… cranberry juice is a good drink by itself, so is prune juice. Or you could serve a combination with either of those as the base and pineapple, orange or lemon juice blended with them. Another good Hallowe'en combination is a mixture of grape juice, cider and ginger ale."

The Citizen Advertiser,
Auburn, New York, October 20, 1938

Pumpkins

The startling fact is that these days in America the vast majority of pumpkins are used for carving, not for eating. In fact, most are grown especially for carving and don't taste very good. But for Native Americans centuries ago, the pumpkin was a lifesaver. Seeds have been found dating back 6,000 years. Apparently, wild pumpkins were too bitter to eat, so the seeds were dried, roasted, and eaten, but once cultivation improved the taste, pumpkins were consumed in every way imaginable—stewed, roasted, baked, boiled. The flowers were added to soups, and dried pumpkins could be made into flour. Strips of dried pumpkin stored well and so helped see the people through the winter. Skins were hollowed out and used as containers, and dried strips woven into mats; and the people continued to roast and eat the seeds, which were thought to have medicinal properties.

Native Americans introduced the Pilgrims to pumpkins, which became pretty much their staple diet. Without them, the Pilgrims might well have been in trouble. Pumpkin pie was said to have graced the tables at the Pilgrims' second Thanksgiving, but it wasn't pie as we know it because there wasn't the wheat to make the pastry. They cut off the top, scooped out the seeds, filled it with milk, eggs, honey, and spices, and baked it in the hot ashes of the fire. The Pilgrims also made an ale from pumpkins, so they were an inventive crowd.

However, come the 20th century, pumpkins were no longer a big feature on many dinner tables, although pumpkin pie had become a Thanksgiving tradition. So the main role pumpkins fulfilled at vintage Hallowe'en celebrations was as decorations—Jack o' lanterns were everywhere by then—and containers for other goodies. "Pumpkins of various sizes should be scooped and scraped to a hollow shell and, lined with wax paper and filled with good things to eat, should be placed in the center of the table." So says Mrs. Herbert B. Linscott. Ruth Edna Kelley is more specific: "For the centerpiece of the table there may be a hollowed pumpkin, filled with apples and nuts and other fruits of harvest, or a pumpkin-chariot drawn by field-mice [presumably of the sugar variety] …in the coach rides a witch."

74

Sweet treats

Popcorn balls have been around since the 1860s, but became a Hallowe'en standard only in the 1950s, for parties and trick-or-treat handouts. Caramel apples, called taffy apples when also rolled in peanuts or another topping, came on the scene in the 1950s, too, and have never waned in popularity, although rarely handed out to doorstep callers after the unfounded scares of the 1960s and 1970s.

Legend has it that candy (toffee) apples were first made by candy maker William Kolb in 1908 in Newark, New Jersey. He dipped some apples in sugar candy (toffee) mixed with red cinnamon for a window display, but ended up selling them, and never looked back. Now this old-fashioned treat is popular all over the world. See opposite for a simple recipe.

caramel apples

The popularity of these Hallowe'en stalwarts doesn't look like fading away. Whether you dip them in a nutty or candy topping or stick with gorgeous plain caramel, munching on one of these treats is part of a traditional Hallowe'en celebration. Since temperature is important in this recipe, you will need a candy thermometer.

1 Put the cream, sugar, and corn syrup (golden syrup) in a large pan and bring to a boil. Reduce the heat, but keep the mixture boiling—it should reach a temperature of 245°F/118°C. Remove the pan from the heat and allow the mixture to settle for a minute or two. Then add the butter and vanilla and stir well.

2 Push the sticks into the washed apples. Swirl them one by one in the caramel mixture, and if you're going to dip them in a topping, do it now. Allow the apples to cool on a sheet of parchment (greaseproof) paper, after which drizzle them with melted chocolate if you like.

You will need

1 cup (240 ml) heavy (double) cream

1 cup (100 g) granulated sugar

¾ cup (250 g) corn syrup (golden syrup)

½ cup (115 g) butter

1 teaspoon vanilla extract

6 popsicle (lollipop) sticks

6 apples of your choice, washed

Optional toppings:
Crushed nuts, Smarties, mini marshmallows, melted chocolate

When witches go riding,
And black cats are seen,
The moon laughs and whispers,
'Tis near Hallowe'en

Anon.

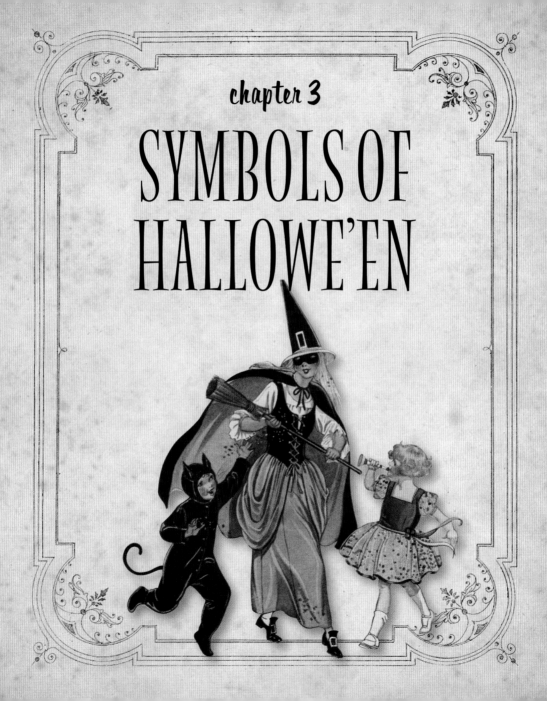

chapter 3

SYMBOLS OF HALLOWE'EN

A THRILLING HALLOWE'EN

Ye Ghost Story

Symbols of Hallowe'en

What images, emblems, tokens, and associations best conjure up the idea of vintage Hallowe'en? In fact, remarkably, these symbols have remained more or less the same through the ages, but the way they are regarded has fundamentally changed. In medieval times, Hallowmas, or Hallowtide, was a religious festival when the saints were honored and the souls of the dead were prayed for. On All Hallows' Eve, vigil was kept in the church; bells were rung; dressing up, so far as it happened at all, was mainly as saints or other figures from the Bible. The mystical and magical were part of life; witches and demons were taken seriously and were to be feared.

In colonial America, observance of the festival was low-key and regional, but over the course of a couple of generations toward the end of the 19th century, all that changed. In Britain by then, Hallowe'en was no longer an exclusively religious occasion. Parties and games, often based on superstition and fortune-telling, had become the norm, and these were the traditions the Irish and Scottish immigrants brought with them. They went down a storm. The old symbolism remained but was adapted and added to, and all things scary became part of the fun.

Black Cats

"Friendly Fairy, Witch, or Fay
Fulfil the
Wish
You wish
to day."

HALLOWE'EN

Cats have long been associated with superstition and religious belief. In ancient Egypt the goddess Bast, took the form of a black cat. The Egyptians honored cats, embalmed their bodies when they died and buried them in mummy cases. In Norse mythology, the goddess Freya rides around in a chariot pulled by two enormous gray cats. The Greek goddess Artemis and the Roman Diana are both associated with cats, while in Japan, the beckoning cat, or "manekineko," symbolizes the goddess of mercy. The story goes that a manekineko saved a passing local ruler by beckoning him into the Gotoku-ji temple just before lightning struck the place where he had been standing. So now, a black beckoning cat symbolizes good health; a gold one symbolizes wealth.

In medieval times, however, the fortune of black cats in particular took a downturn in parallel to the rise in the belief that witches were in league with the Devil. Black cats took the role of witches' familiars—creatures that provided a link to the satanic master. Although other animals, including owls, bats, and toads, could be familiars, a black cat was the one witches were most likely to turn themselves into—and back again—should the need arise.

Cat Sith

In Celtic mythology, the Cat Sith was a large black cat with a white spot on its chest that haunted the Scottish Highlands and, occasionally, parts of Ireland. This fairy creature was no cuddly, purring feline. It often appeared with back arched and fur standing on end in an attitude either threatening or defensive. At Samhain, people would leave out saucers of milk to avoid the Cat Sith's curse, which would cause their cows' milk to dry up.

Another tale has it that the Cat Sith was not a fairy at all but a witch who could change from human to cat form and back eight times. On the ninth time, the witch could shapeshift no more, and remained a black cat. Well, they do say a cat has nine lives!

A MERRY Hallowe'en

TO YOU
ON
HALLOWEEN

Hallmark

84

Black cats and luck

The meaning of a black cat crossing your path depended on where you lived. In most parts of America it was, and is if you are of a superstitious turn of mind, bad luck, although black and white, or gray, was the opposite. In Britain, a black cat signified good luck. In fact, if a black cat turned up on your doorstep in Scotland, that was a sign of coming prosperity. An old English proverb says, "Whenever the cat of the house is black, the lasses of lovers will no lack," and in some parts of England, a black cat given as a wedding gift was thought to bring the bride good luck.

Some other old superstitions persist. In Germany, if a black cat crosses your path right to left, that's bad luck; if it crosses left to right, that's good luck. In southern Europe, it's bad luck whichever way it chooses to go.

On board ship, black cats are good luck, but if one mews and seems bad-tempered, the coming voyage will be hard. If a sailor's family keeps a black cat at home and looks after it well, fair weather at sea is ensured.

If you see three black cats, one after the other, that's good luck. It's also good luck if a black cat sits down by your side or rubs up against your leg or greets you in some way, especially if it jumps up into your lap. If it turns away, that's bad luck, and if it runs away, that means you have a secret and it will soon be revealed. And if a black cat sits beside you and yawns, you may think it's just tired, or bored, but what it really means is that an opportunity will soon come your way and you have to keep your wits about you to be sure not to miss it.

A story that crops up from time to time is that a 13th-century pope, Gregory IX, was responsible for linking black cats to Devil worship, leading to their long-term mass extermination and thus, indirectly, a pandemic of the plague. The feared Black Death certainly swept through Europe in the 14th century, wiping out approximately a third of the population. A hundred years or so earlier, Gregory had allegedly issued an edict, *Vox in Rama*, condemning a devilish cult that seemed to be flourishing in Germany at the time and describing in detail how Satan took the form of a black cat in the sect's rites. This was enough for all black cats to be condemned as incarnations of the Devil. The logic goes that, as a consequence, with fewer cats to prey on them, black rats were able to go forth and multiply in their millions. The rats carried the fleas that caused the plague, and thus the infection spread like wildfire. However, no trace of *Vox in Rama* apparently survives, and whether it ever existed at all is open to doubt. Without any real evidence to support it, this story involves too many assumptions to be taken at face value and perhaps can be better regarded as medieval urban myth.

But such tales have a way of permeating the popular mind so that, after a while, they are taken as fact, despite being nothing of the sort. Thus hearsay and legend can be passed down through generations and evolve into what may come to be regarded as common knowledge. Perhaps that's why black cats retained their devilish connotation for several hundred years.

However that may be, the Pilgrims brought their superstitions about black cats and witchcraft with them when they settled in

A MERRY HALLOWE'EN

"For Ways that are dark and tricks that are vain" Watch out!

Massachusetts in 1620. Other immigrants, especially from Germany, Holland, Haiti, and Africa, brought their own customs, often also involving black cats and sorcery. So by the time Hallowe'en was adopted wholeheartedly in the late 19th and early 20th centuries as a great excuse for a party, black cats and witches had become as inseparable as Toto and Dorothy. The folklore had melded, and although how it was observed continued to vary from region to region, witches and their black cats had become an integral part of it all. And as the years went by, many of those fearsome black cats had a tendency to turn into unbelievably cute kittens.

HALLOWE'EN

DESIGN COPYRIGHTED BY RAPHAEL TUCK & SONS CO. TUCK

88

Witches

Back at the turn of the last century, Hallowe'en witches were not the provocative sirens of today. Vintage witches hark back to the days of flowing black cloaks, pointed hats and chins, warty noses, flying broomsticks, and steaming cauldrons. These are the traditional witches of fairy tales. One superstition said that if you want to meet a witch, you should put your clothes on inside out and walk backward on October 31, but there was really no need to go to those lengths because they were everywhere—on cards, adorning houses, wandering the streets, at parties, parading through town.

Witches have been with us since time immemorial. In olden times, they were thought of as wise healers, but gradually, as beliefs and superstitions changed, they came to be regarded much more negatively and were denounced as heretics by the Church. Up until the last few hundred years, belief in them was common and those people thought to be witches commanded fear or respect, depending on your point of view. They were said to practice magic, for good or evil, and indulge in black arts. Anyone suspected of witchcraft was hunted down. Paranoia against witches was at its height in Europe from the 1300s to the 1600s, and many ordinary folk, especially women, with knowledge of herbs and healing, were persecuted. In America, notorious witch trials took place at Salem, Massachusetts, in 1692, when 150 men and women were imprisoned and many died, one way or another. This outbreak of supposed witchery was eventually put down to mass hysteria, local rivalries, and possibly a toxic fungus that can be found in cereal crops and causes muscle spasms, vomiting, and hallucinations. Rye bread was a staple of the settlers' diet at the time.

By the 1900s, witches had lost their fearful aura and metamorphosed into the deliciously scary Hallowe'en favorites of many children intent on dressing up and party-going in the spirit of the times.

A gypsy flame is on the hearth,
Sign of this carnival of mirth.
Through the dun fields
and from the glade
Flash merry folk in
masquerade—
It is the witching Hallowe'en.

From "Hallowe'en" by A.F. Murray, first published in *Harper's Weekly*, October 30, 1909

Hey-how for Hallowe'en!
A' the witches tae be seen,
Some are black, an' some green,
Hey-how for Hallowe'en.

Old Scottish rhyme

No one seems to know why
Hallowe'en witches were often
depicted as being green. One theory
is that it originated as recently as
1900, with the publication of The
Wizard of Oz *and the famously*
green Wicked Witch of the West.

witch costume

Witches have never lost their magic at Hallowe'en, and as trick-or-treaters they remain as popular as ever. Watch your child cast her spell in this lovely costume, and charm candy from neighbors' front porches and into her bucket by the armful. You will need to buy a long-sleeved black top and stripy tights, but the rest is homemade, in true vintage Hallowe'en style.

You will need

Templates on pages 140–41

52 x 55 in. (130 x 137 cm) each of black net and purple net for the skirt

51 in. (127 cm) ribbon 1½ in. (4 cm) wide for the skirt waistband

82 in. (205 cm) ribbon ¼ in. (5 mm) wide for the skirt

22 x 48 in. (54 x 120 cm) black felt for the hat

Matching sewing threads

Pins

High-tack craft glue

30 x 45 in. (76 x 112 cm) black fabric for the cloak

60 in. (150 cm) velvet ribbon ¾ in. (2 cm) wide for the cloak

Scrap of gold felt for buckles on the shoes

Black sneakers

Black top and striped leggings, tights, or socks (to complete costume)

1 Fold one net piece in half and in half again so it is 55 x 13 in. (137 x 32.5 cm). Sew running stitch along the long folded edge (the one with no raw edges). Pull the thread to gather the net to 24 in. (60 cm) wide; check the fit on your child. Repeat for the other piece.

2 Pin and baste the two skirts together along the top. Now pin and stitch the wider ribbon along the top. Fold 12 in. (30 cm) lengths of ribbon in half and sew the folded ends to the ribbon waistband. Cut along the folds at the bottom of the skirt, then cut V-shapes from the net on this edge, cutting each layer separately to make a jagged lower edge.

3 To make the hat, cut out a top and brim from black felt using templates on pages 140–41. Fold the top in half, right sides together, matching the long edges. Pin and machine stitch a ⅜ in. (1 cm) seam down the long edge. Turn right side out.

4 Pin the felt brim to the bottom edge of the hat top. Hand sew all the way around using small, tidy overhand stitches. Glue a length of narrow ribbon around the hat to decorate it, overlapping the ends.

5 To make the cloak, you may need to adjust the size of the black fabric, depending on how tall your child is (don't forget to allow for the seams). Press under ⅜ in. (1 cm) on the two short edges and one long edge, and then press under another ⅜ in. (1 cm). Pin and stitch. Press under ⅜ in. (1 cm) on the remaining raw edge and then another ¾ in. (2 cm). Pin and stitch, forming a channel.

6 For the ties, thread the velvet ribbon through the channel using a safety pin. Pull the ribbon through until the neck edge is gathered up and the ends of the ribbon are the same length for tying in a big bow.

7 For the shoes, cut two rectangles from gold felt and then cut out a smaller rectangle from the middle of each one. Glue them onto plain black sneakers to look like big buckles.

Ghosts

Ghosts, specters, spirits—belief in them seems to be common in varying degrees to almost every culture. In Celtic lore, Samhain, the fall fire festival, was their time. This was when the souls of the dead returned to Earth, and how those still living reacted depended on whether they wanted to attract the spirits or hide from them.

A HALLOWEEN BIRTHDAY WISH FOR YOU

*From ghoulies
and ghosties
And long-leggedy
beasties
And things that go
bump in the night,
Good Lord, deliver us!*

Traditional Scottish rhyme

The spirits of your own ancestors may have had nothing but friendly intent, but others abroad that night may have had other ideas. If passing ghosts found no offering set out for them, the household would be inviting bad luck for the coming year—early shades of trick-or-treating, perhaps!

With the creation of Hallowmas—All Hallows' Eve, All Saints' Day, and All Souls' Day—the link with the dead was cemented. This was a time to be praying for the souls of those who had passed on, and concentration on death and what is to come does tend to focus the mind on matters spiritual.

In colonial days, when the observance of Hallowe'en was by no means universal across America, the telling of ghost stories was part of what was by today's standards a rather muted occasion. The custom has continued through all the Hallowe'en changes and adaptations right up until the present day, so a vintage Hallowe'en has to include a good ghost story, and if possible a visit to a haunted house. There's no need to be scared—all the apparitions you see will most likely be of the store-bought variety.

The likelihood of seeing a ghost that doesn't resemble someone dressed up in a bedsheet with two holes for eyes is fairly remote, and even if you did happen to come across one, all you have to do is walk around it nine times and it will disappear.

Victorian tales of specters, phantoms, and general eeriness are best read aloud by firelight or candlelight. Atmosphere is all! Charles Dickens wrote some wonderful ghostly tales, including *The Trial for Murder* and *The Signal-Man*. Robert Louis Stevenson's *The Body-Snatcher*, Jerome K. Jerome's *The Man of Science*, or Mrs Henry Wood's *Reality or Delusion?* are guaranteed to scare the assembled listeners witless. The legends of Bloody Mary and Black Aggie are always good for retelling, if goriness is required, as is the story of the Bell witch. In the early 1800s, Tennessee farmer John Bell's family were persecuted by a malicious supernatural being, and this malevolent spirit revisits his descendants from time to time. *A Hallowe'en Wraith* by William Black, on the other hand, has a happy ending and so stands a better chance of sending the children to bed in a less jumpy frame of mind.

SKULLS AND SKELETONS

Since Hallowmas focused on death, it's not so surprising that the imagery of skeletons and skulls became part of the Hallowe'en tradition. The connection may well go back even farther to Samhain, when the veil thinned between the living and the spirit world and the souls of the dead returned to Earth. Apparently, the Celts believed that the skull was where the soul resided.

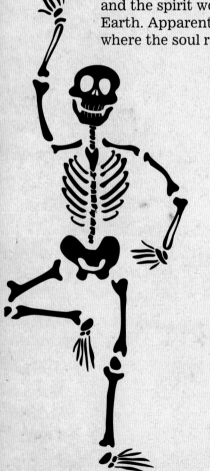

In some parts of the world, an annual Festival of the Dead coincides with Hallowe'en, the Mexican Dias de los Muertos, for example. November 1 is the Day of the Innocents, or children, the Day of the Dead is November 2, and the celebrations start on October 31. The festival is thought to have Aztec origins, and became intermingled with Hallowmas after the Spanish arrived and tried to convert the local populace to their own religious beliefs.

Have you seen the ghost of John?
Long white bones and the rest all gone,
Ooh, ooh, wouldn't it be chilly with
no skin on?

Traditional rhyme

Kite festival

In Guatemala in Central America, October 31 is marked by releasing large, elaborate kites, if possible from a hill overlooking a cemetery. The kites are flimsy, and the crowd watch them being wrecked by the elements. The idea is that this should encourage them to reflect on the transitory nature of life.

The festival's rituals are much the same now as they were a hundred and more years ago. Skeleton costumes are still all the rage. Graves are cleaned, tidied, and beautified. Altars are set up, often outside in the street as well as indoors, and adorned with marigolds, photographs of the dead, some of their favorite things, sugar skulls, and other food, including specially baked bread, sometimes decorated with representations of bones. The focus is on remembering family and friends with love and affection, and the atmosphere is happy rather than scary, despite the preponderance of skulls and skeletons on the streets and in parades. The festival is really a celebration of life, and in Mexico, they know how to party.

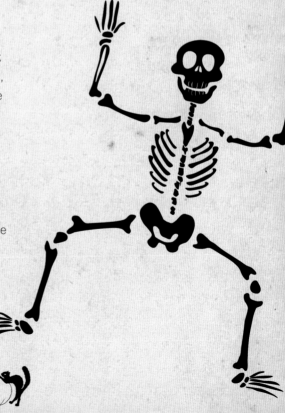

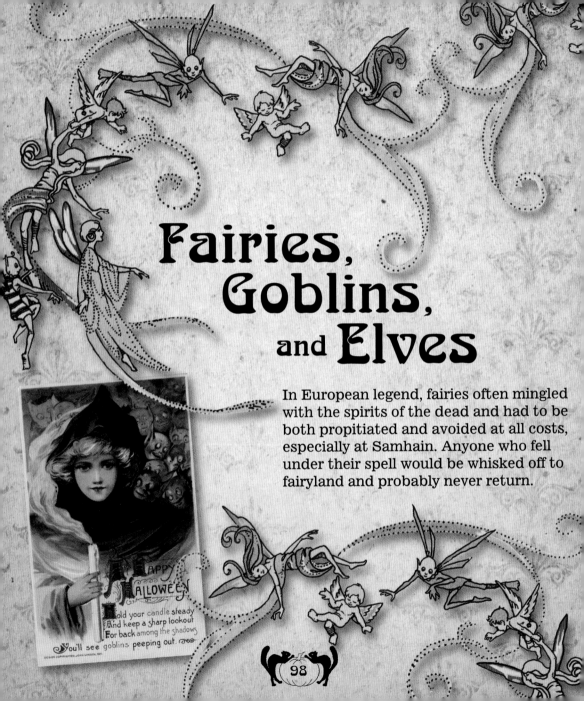

Fairies, Goblins, and Elves

In European legend, fairies often mingled with the spirits of the dead and had to be both propitiated and avoided at all costs, especially at Samhain. Anyone who fell under their spell would be whisked off to fairyland and probably never return.

HAPPY HALLOWEEN

Hold your candle steady
And keep a sharp lookout
For back among the shadows
You'll see goblins peeping out.

DESIGN COPYRIGHTED, JOHN WINSCH, 1911.

98

Native American myths are full of fairies, goblins, and elves, from manitous and trolls to marauding pukwudgies. Victorian fairy tales, as set down by the Brothers Grimm among others, were principally based on deeply rooted folklore, but gradually, the more sinister parts of the tales were left out and happy endings became the order of the day. Traditional fairy tales of long ago and far away became a magical part of childhood and, since fairyland is all-pervading, why wouldn't fairies in all their guises be part of Hallowe'en?

I hope the goblins
Pass you by
But if they catch you
Don't you cry.

Rhyme from an old postcard

Pixie, kobold, elf, and sprite,
All are on their rounds tonight;
In the wan moon's silver ray,
Thrives their helter-skelter play.

From "Hallowe'en" by Joel Benton (1832–1911), published in *Harper's Weekly*, October 31, 1896

'Tis night when
Goblin, Elf, and Fay,
Come dancing in their best array
To prank and royster on the way,
And ease the troubled soul.

From "Hallowe'en" by John Kendrick Bangs (1862–1922), published in *Harper's Weekly*, November 5, 1910

BATS AND SPIDERS

Bonfires, which continued to be a feature of Hallowmas, even after the Celtic fall fire festival had been superseded, attracted insects to their light, which in turn attracted bats in search of dinner. Bats' connection with vampires was well established by popular 19th-century gothic novels, especially the masterpiece of the genre, Bram Stoker's *Dracula* (published in 1897), and once bats became a Hallowe'en must-have, vampires soon followed. After them came zombies, werewolves, and any other horror-story stalwart that took the holiday fancy. What fun to dress up as an early equivalent of Shaun of the Dead and scare the neighbors silly—unless they were out doing the same thing!

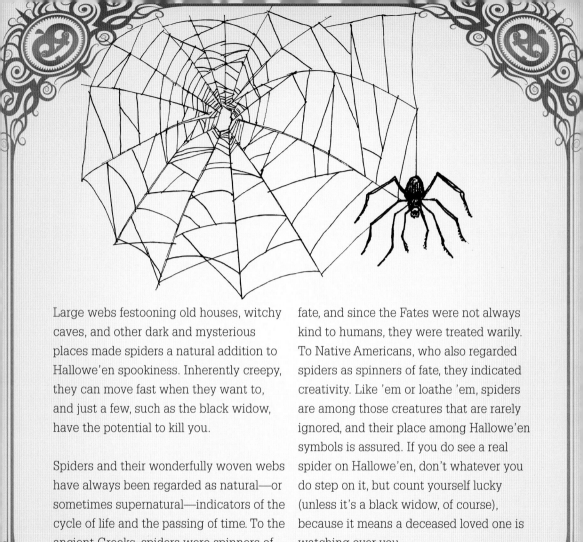

Large webs festooning old houses, witchy caves, and other dark and mysterious places made spiders a natural addition to Hallowe'en spookiness. Inherently creepy, they can move fast when they want to, and just a few, such as the black widow, have the potential to kill you.

Spiders and their wonderfully woven webs have always been regarded as natural—or sometimes supernatural—indicators of the cycle of life and the passing of time. To the ancient Greeks, spiders were spinners of fate, and since the Fates were not always kind to humans, they were treated warily. To Native Americans, who also regarded spiders as spinners of fate, they indicated creativity. Like 'em or loathe 'em, spiders are among those creatures that are rarely ignored, and their place among Hallowe'en symbols is assured. If you do see a real spider on Hallowe'en, don't whatever you do step on it, but count yourself lucky (unless it's a black widow, of course), because it means a deceased loved one is watching over you.

Harvest

Quite a few of the symbols of vintage Hallowe'en are to do with the harvest, harking back perhaps to the days when fall fire festivals marked the end of the old year and were a means of both offering thanks to the powers that be for the year's produce and seeking protection for the coming winter. Hallowe'en scarecrows carried on the idea of protection. They symbolized guarding against crop failure as much as against hungry birds. Corn shocks and, later, corn candy fell in with the harvest theme.

On Hallowe'en the gobble-uns
May seize and carry you off to their den;
So you'd best try hard to obtain the guard
Of Kernel Corn and his husk-y men.

Rhyme from an old postcard

USE SLEEPER'S
CRESCENT GLOSS
AND CORN STARCH.

Colors of Hallowe'en

*Black: night, dark days of winter,
death, witches, black cats, bats, spiders*

*Orange: the color of fall, harvest,
pumpkins, Jack o' lanterns, firelight*

Purple: supernatural, magic, shadows

Green: witches, goblins, monsters

Red: blood, danger

White: ghosts, ghouls, skeletons

Turn your boots toward the street
Leave your garters on your feet,
Put your stockings on your head,
You'll dream of the one you're going to wed.

Traditional rhyme

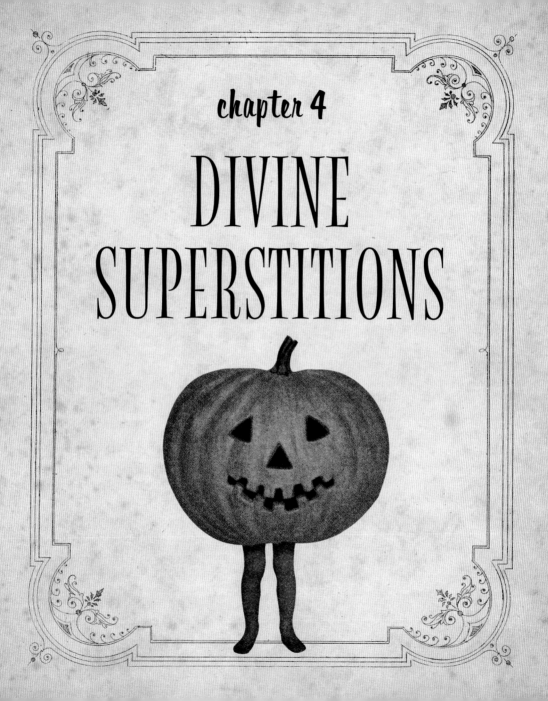

chapter 4

DIVINE SUPERSTITIONS

Divine Superstitions

How is it that quaint, essentially rural, folk customs from Ireland and Scotland survived hundreds of years into the 20th century, and were adopted with such enthusiasm in America?

Through the centuries, Hallowe'en rituals and superstitions evolved along surprisingly similar lines in different areas. Rather than protection from unknown forces, their purpose mostly became divination, foretelling the future, especially concerning romance and marriage. The various charms and spells that were practiced in 19th and 20th-century America were being pursued with equal relish in 18th-century Scotland and Ireland. Perhaps it's only natural to wonder what the future holds. As Robert Burns wrote in the prelude to his poem "Hallowe'en," published in 1785, "The passion of prying into futurity makes a striking part of the history of human nature in its rude state, in all ages and nations."

Divinations that were a matter of interpretation—foretelling future happiness with nut burning, or pulling kale stalks, for instance—were delightful if you could decipher them in your favor, and merely disappointing if you couldn't, but others would have been terrifying if they had actually worked. However, whether anyone ever really saw disembodied, handsome faces smiling back at them in the glass, or witnessed a phantom coming to turn a wet shirt that was spread out to dry, must be open to doubt. Maybe that's why these games, charms, superstitions—call them what you will—carried on for so long. Since the chances of a specter appearing were nil (or close to nil—after all, you never know!), you could enjoy the shivers and spookiness in the sure and certain knowledge that nothing ghostly, or ghastly, would occur.

Robert Burns

(1759–96)

Scotland's national poet was the son of a tenant farmer, the eldest child of seven. He was educated by his father, by local teachers when enough money could be scraped together to pay for a few lessons, and by himself. Growing up in a poor farming community gave him an insight into peasant life and lore, and he drew on these for much of his poetry. In "Hallowe'en," published in 1785, possibly inspired by fellow poet John Mayne (1759–1836), he featured many of the long-practiced customs of All Hallows' Eve. Burns also collected and preserved a number of Scottish folk songs. The hardships and tough manual labor of his early life are thought to have weakened his health and contributed, along with later riotous living, to his early death, at the age of 37.

By the Cards your Fortune I'll tell
Be it Hearts, Spades, Diamonds or Clubs
For o'er your Fate I'll ponder Well
And illustrate Hallowe'en Dubs.

APPLES

Apples and Hallowe'en go back a long way. In Celtic lore, the apple symbolized fruitfulness, and Druid wands were made of either yew or apple wood, so it's entirely possible that apples had a role to play in the festival of Samhain. If you cut an apple in half horizontally, the core resembles a pentagram—a five-pointed star—and the Celts regarded the pentagram as a symbol of fertility. So perhaps the idea of finding your future partner through divination using apples and seeds stems from this in some convoluted way.

Ducking for Apples

In any case, it's fair to say that at least since the Romans celebrated the festival of Pomona in Britain in the early years of the first millennium, apples have featured at this time of year, as a symbol of the harvest and, latterly, as a convenient ingredient of Hallowe'en games and fortune-telling.

Bobbing for Apples

This is one of the earliest apple games, and by the early 20th century there were several versions of it, all starting with plenty of apples floating in a tub of water. No use of hands was allowed. You always had to catch one with your teeth—or sometimes, in the interests of hygiene, with a fork that you dropped or manipulated with your mouth—and often the game ended there. If several people bobbed at the same time, the first one

to succeed would be the first one married. And if a girl put an apple she had caught by bobbing under her pillow, she would likely dream of her future lover.

In another version, there were two tubs and the apples had names attached, girls' names in one tub, boys' in the other. The name on the apple you managed to catch would be the name of your future partner.

In probably the oldest version of the game, some say a survivor of Celtic origin, once you'd caught your apple, you were required to peel it in one long strip, swing the peel around your head three times, east to west, and throw it over your shoulder. If it formed an initial on landing—and you were allowed to use your imagination—that would be the initial of your true love.

In Scotland, the game was, and still is, known as dooking for apples, in parts of England as apple ducking, and in Ireland as snap apple, although, confusingly, snap apple is also the name of a different game.

No time is this for tear or sob,
Or other woes our joys to rob,
But time for Pippin and for Bob,
And Jack-o'-lantern gay.

From "Hallowe'en" by John Kendrick Bangs (1862–1922),
published in *Harper's Weekly*, November 5, 1910

On November 1, 2008, in the Scottish town of Peebles, 67 people dooked (bobbed) for apples at the same time, setting a world record in the process. The participants included the local Member of Parliament and a town councillor, and the tubs were filled with water by the local fire service. The mass dooking was part of a Hallowe'en week that also included a parade and fancy-dress events in the true spirit of guising—so no sign of old Hallowe'en customs fading in that part of Scotland.

May you always get the apple you want!

Nuts

Nuts, along with apples, have a long association with Hallowe'en. Hazelnuts and chestnuts seem to be the favorites, and burning them often featured. A couple would put a nut each into the fire, possibly on a shovel, and if the nuts burned together, that meant the two would remain faithful to each other. If one nut cracked or leaped up, the person whose nut it was would be unfaithful; if one nut was engulfed in flame, that person had deep feelings for someone else. Another nut-burning game involved putting several nuts onto the fire, having named them after various potential lovers. The first one that popped bore the name of your true love: "If he loves me, pop and fly; If he hates me, burn and die."

Nutshell boats

Each person adopted half a nutshell for a boat and put a tiny candle in it. Once all the candles were lit, the boats were floated in a tub of water and how they behaved indicated their owner's future life. For instance, if a boat clung to the sides of the tub, its owner would lead a quiet life. If two persisted in floating together, well, the result was clear. Onlookers could ruffle the water with their hands to encourage movement. The last candle to go out indicated the person who would be first to marry. The person whose candle went out first would probably remain single.

Needles could also be floated in water, instead of nutshells, and if two stuck together, those namesakes would be lovers. If more than two clung together, the results could be interesting!

> *Bring forth the raisins and the nuts—*
> *Tonight All-Hallows specter struts*
> *Along the moonlit way.*
>
> From "Hallowe'en" by John Kendrick Bangs (1862–1922), published in *Harper's Weekly*, November 5, 1910

Candles

Candle flames provide an atmospheric light, soft and romantic or shadowy and spooky, depending on location and mood. If you decide to include candle games in your vintage Hallowe'en celebration, do be aware of the fire risk and take sensible precautions.

Jumping over lighted candles seems to have been a favorite—maybe it was a substitute for leaping over the dying flames of a bonfire, and certainly a little less daunting. In one game, twelve lighted candles, representing the months of the year, were spaced out in a row. Players took turns to leap over them, while at the same time attempting to blow them out. The first person to extinguish a flame would marry in the month that the candle represented.

Another version used just one candle. If the person jumping over it managed to blow it out, that meant a bad year was on the way. If it remained alight, the leaper had a good year to look forward to—which seems a pretty good reason not to try too hard. Revolving a stick with a lighted candle fixed to it while others tried to blow it out may have had a similar significance, but it seems an odd way to play a game, with the incentive not to succeed. Perhaps the rules have been skewed in the telling and, in reality, it was the other way around.

Outdoor Charms

Hallowe'en's connection with the harvest means that some divinations were bound to involve crops. Beside apples and nuts, those that featured most prominently were cabbages or kale, oats, and hemp, requiring the seeker of future knowledge to go outside to perform the rituals.

Unmarried lads and lasses would go to the cabbage or kale field and, blindfolded or with eyes shut, select a plant to pull up. The size and shape of the stalk—from tall and straight through slim and crooked, to old and past its best—indicated the character of the person they were destined to marry. The earth clinging to the root was significant, too—plenty of it could mean wealth—and if the cabbage came up easily, a partner would be easily wooed. Couples would take part in the ritual, hoping to gain an insight into how their future married life would turn out.

Another version suggests that if a girl slipped off to steal a cabbage from a nearby patch, she would see her future husband as she pulled it up, or meet him on the way home. And if that should fail, she should balance said cabbage, or at least its stalk, over a door because she

would be sure to marry whomever it fell on. Oat stalks had a different connotation. According to Robert Burns, the young people "go to the barnyard and pull each, at three different times, a stalk of oats. If the third stalk wants the 'top-pickle,' that is, the grain at the top of the stalk, the party in question will come to the marriage-bed anything but a maid." Burns added a whole string of helpful footnotes to his poem "Hallowe'en," which was written in dialect. This one was to do with Nelly and Rab "kiutlin in the fause-house"—read the poem! Later, they burn nuts and canoodle in a quiet nook, so their story has a happy ending.

When it came to hemp seed, Burns was quite precise. "Steal out, unperceived, and sow a handful of hemp-seed, harrowing it with anything you can conveniently draw after you. Repeat now and then: 'Hemp-seed I saw [sow]

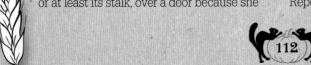

thee, hemp-seed, I saw thee; and him (or her) that is to be my true love, come after me and pou [pull] thee.' Look over your left shoulder, and you will see the appearance of the person invoked, in the attitude of pulling hemp." Using old Hallowe'en customs as a reason for sowing hemp seed today may not be such a good idea, or cut much ice with the authorities, since this is the marijuana plant. Although nothing to do with crops or harvest, the shirt-sleeve charm nevertheless involved going outside. You had to find a place with flowing water where three estates met—after dark on Hallowe'en. Perhaps that was why this was not a solitary task and it was fine to go as a group. Once you had found an appropriate place, you soaked your left sleeve in the water, and hurried back so that the shirt didn't dry on the way. The next step was to hang the still wet shirt to dry in front of the fire and go to bed. Around midnight a phantom resembling your future spouse would come to turn the shirt to dry the other side. Presumably, you had to make up a bed in the room with the fire, or you would miss the phantom, which was the point of it all.

The yarn test

In Robert Burns' poem, "Hallowe'en," Merran has her sights set on Andrew Bell and tries her luck at a charm involving a ball of blue yarn. She creeps out to the kiln by herself and throws the yarn into the pot, keeping hold of the end so that she can wind it up again. What should have happened is that when the ball was nearly rewound, the yarn should have become taut with something, or someone, holding the thread. Merran would then demand, "Who holds?" and from the kiln-pot a voice would name her future spouse—Andrew Bell as she hoped. However, when

"... something held within the pat [pot], Good Lord! but she was quaukin! [quaking] But whether 'twas the deil [devil] himsel, Or whether 'twas a bauk-en' [shadow], Or whether it was Andrew Bell, She did na wait on talkin to spier [ask] that night."
—and who can blame her?"
In America, the yarn was thrown into a barn so it unraveled. Whoever was doing the throwing kept hold of the end and a future lover would appear to help wind it up again. In Ireland, the yarn was thrown out of the window and you had to listen carefully to hear the answer to the question "Who holds?" whispered on the night air.

INDOOR GAMES

More sedate parlor games were enjoyed, too. Letters were carved on a pumpkin, for instance, and participants, blindfolded, invited to stick strong pins into it. The nearest initial to your pin was the initial of whatever the game had been designated to foretell—future partner, country or county for next year's vacation, winner of the Derby.
A slightly more boisterous variation was for the pumpkin to be suspended, twisted a few times, and then let go. All the players attacked it with their pins at the same time, hopefully missing one another.

Bowls of water seem to feature heavily in Hallowe'en games, which may be fortuitous with so many candles around. Beside apple bobbing and nutshell boats, one idea was to wrap fortunes in aluminum foil or orange peel and float them on water laced with alcohol to make it burn. Guests would try to grab one at random, which sounds a little scary, considering the water was on fire. The person who grabbed the fortune deemed to be the best would meet his/her future partner within a year.

If the burning water game didn't appeal, you could always try the three balls of meal or maize flour. A slip of paper with the name of a potential suitor written on it was tucked into

each one (a different name on each slip!) and all three were dropped into a bowl of water. The first one that rose to the surface held the lucky man's name.

It's a
HALLOWEEN
PARTY

Shapes in water

The white of an egg left in a glass half filled with water for 24 hours will fold into all sorts of shapes, and if you knew how to read tea leaves, you could use the same skill with the egg white to predict the future.

That skill was not required, although it might have helped, to discover the occupation of your future partner. All you had to do was drop molten lead or wax into a dish of cold water to see what shape it made: a horse meant you were destined to marry a dragoon, a helmet meant a policeman, a round shape with a spike meant a sailor, a cow meant a farmer—but it was all a matter of interpretation. In "Halloween, or Chrissie's Fate," a story published in *Century Magazine* in 1871, one of the first charms the girls try is the molten-lead trick. Aunt Jeannette observes while her niece Kitty and her friends heat an old iron spoon and take turns with the molten metal.

"The sharp hiss and splutter brought an immediate 'cloud of witnesses' and a puzzled silence, which was soon broken by merry queries.

'Why, Madge, it looks like a pulpit—hope you're not going to marry a missionary!'

'Indeed, no, dear; it is much more like a beer mug. Guess it's a German student.'

'Well, it's obscure enough to be anything,' said Madge, in a tone of dissatisfaction. 'I'm not one whit wiser for that venture. Who'll spoon next?'

With 'I believe I'm your next neighbor,' Netta Fane consulted the fiery oracle; and peals of laughter arose as one and another traced resemblances, until Kitty sprang from her post with flushed face and burning fingers, and the declaration that it was time for something new.

'I conclude from this trick that we shall just all marry tinkers…'"

Prophetic Dreams

To dream of what the future may hold, go out of the front door backward, gather some grass or dust, wrap it in paper, and put it under your pillow.

Remove the yolk from a hardboiled egg, half fill the cavity with salt, and eat it before going to bed. Alternatively, eat a salty herring in three bites. Don't drink anything. Then, in your dreams you will see your future mate bringing you water—a thirst-induced hallucination, perhaps?

If, after consuming a concoction of grated walnuts, hazelnuts, and nutmeg mixed with butter and sugar before bed, you dream of gold, your future husband will be rich; if you dream of noise, he will be a tradesman; if you dream of a thunderstorm, he will be a traveler. If you merely suffer from indigestion, it hasn't worked!

Bay leaves under the pillow give a man dreams of his lover; for a woman it's rosemary.

Eating some dry bread before bed promotes undisturbed sleep and wish fulfillment.

If you bake a dumb-cake and eat a slice before bed while walking backward (again!), your future partner will appear in your dreams. To make a dumb-cake, several people knead the mixture, made with flour, eggs, and salt, with their left thumbs while not saying a word.

A FACTOR OF THREE

"Take three dishes, put clean water in one, foul water in another, and leave the third empty; blindfold a person and lead him to the hearth where the dishes are ranged; he (or she) dips the left hand; if by chance in the clean water, the future (husband or) wife will come to the bar of matrimony a maid; if in the foul, a widow; if in the empty dish, it foretells, with equal certainty, no marriage at all. It is repeated three times, and every time the arrangement of dishes is altered." So said Robert Burns in his footnotes to "Hallowe'en."

In the poem, old Uncle John is so irate at choosing the empty dish three times, he hurls them all on the fire.

In America, four dishes were set out containing earth, water, a ring, and a rag. The blindfolded participant who chose the dish containing earth would soon be divorced, the person who chose the water would embark on a trip across the sea, and the one who chose the ring was off to the altar pronto. The rag meant no marriage at all.

In Leinster in the days of old, I wis,
There was no maiden of the countryside
But on All Hallows (such a night as this!)
In Love's dim chancery her fortune tried.
The bursting nut upon the hearth she plied;
Or, while a lighted candle she would bear,
Gazed in her glass with eyes intent and wide;
Or, with weird mutterings, like a witch's prayer,
She sowed three rows of nothing on empty air!

From "The Enchanted Ring, A Tale of Hallowe'en" by Edith Matilda Thomas (1854–1925), published in *The Delineator Magazine* in November 1900. Leinster is a province in Ireland. Intriguing to know what the "weird mutterings" might have been, and the significance of sowing "three rows of nothing on empty air."

"In order, on the clean hearth-stane,
The luggies [dishes] three are ranged;
An' ev'ry time great care is ta'en
To see them duly changed:
Auld uncle John, wha wedlock's joys
Sin' Mar's year did desire,
Because he gat the toom
[empty] dish thrice,
He heav'd them on the fire
In wrath that night."

From "Hallowe'en" (1785) by Robert Burns. Mar's year probably refers to 1715, when the Earl of Mar fought (and lost) a battle against George I's army in the first Jacobite rebellion.

Hallowe'en superstitions

- Finish your journey by sunset if you don't want to run into wandering spirits.

- Salt was thought to be a witch repellant, so if you're out and about, carry a piece of bread crossed with salt to be on the safe side.

- A flickering candle flame indicates the presence of a visiting soul. Knocking over a candle is very bad luck (especially if a fire results!)

- Anyone born on All Hallows' Eve has the gift of second sight.

- Catch a falling leaf for good luck and good health during the winter.

- At the stroke of midnight on All Hallows' Eve, observe a minute or twos silence to show respect for visiting spirits.

- Brooming the house from front to back sweeps all the past year's troubles away and leaves it ready for whatever the new year may bring.

- Listen to the wind to hear whispers about the future.

- Prepare a meal in silence and eat it at midnight, also in silence, if you want a spirit to join you at the table. This is known as a dumb supper.

- A girl deciding whether to accept a proposal of marriage should take three hairs from a cat's tail (good luck with that!), wrap them loosely in paper, and place them under the doormat. If in the morning the hairs seem to form a Y or an N pattern, she will know what to reply.

O bliss of the collector... no one has a greater sense of well-being than... a collector

Walter Benjamin (1892–1940), literary critic
and philosopher

chapter 5

COLLECTIBLES

Collectibles

Once Hallowe'en had become a fixture, and parties, whether community gatherings or private shindigs, had become the norm, it soon became possible to buy most of the accessories associated with such occasions, rather than making them yourself. New ideas created new trends and new demands. Manufacturers rushed to produce postcards, greetings cards, paper and table decorations, figurines, and noisemakers, and such items are now highly collectible. Costumes were mainly homemade, and authentic prewar outfits are much sought-after.

Genuine vintage memorabilia are often expensive, depending on their rarity, but these days several companies offer beautifully produced, vintage-style decorations and table settings at reasonable prices. For a vintage Hallowe'en, it may be a good idea to go for some of these, even if you also have some cherished originals to display. (If these are delicate and you're going to worry about them being handled, it might be better to keep them away from the heat of the partying.)

Postcards, greetings cards, party invitations, and giftwrap all show the style of the times, reflecting the changing nature of Hallowe'en from dark and grotesque to whimsical family fun. Cute black kittens, chubby children in red capes, smiling ghosts, and rather bemused-looking owls sum it up. The scarecrows and Jack o' lanterns are welcoming, scary faces or not, and even the spiders and bats manage to seem friendly.

HALLOWE'EN GREETING

Hallowe'en
Greetings.

Frances Brundage

Design Copyright 1910 by Frances Brundage.

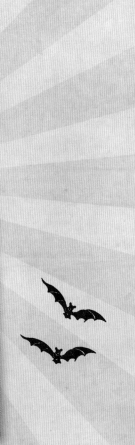

124

POSTCARDS

Hallowe'en postcard rhymes

We, the pumpkins and the old black cats
The witch, the moon and the bats
Send greetings on Hallowe'en.

On Hallowe'en the thing you must do
Is pretend that nothing can frighten you
An' if somethin' scares you and you want to run
Jus' let on like it's Hallowe'en fun.

One idea that really came into vogue was sending Hallowe'en postcards. For a while it became as ritualized a part of the holiday as sending greetings cards at Christmas. The enthusiasm for Hallowe'en postcards lasted from 1905 to around 1918. Bewitching illustrations and charming rhymes on beautifully produced cards (mostly printed in Germany before the First World War) landed in mailboxes throughout the country, adding to the growing sense of anticipation as the holiday approached.

This creativity was allowed to flourish because from 1898, under the Private Mailing Card Act, private publishers were allowed to produce what they were required to call "souvenir cards." Prior to that, the United States Postal Service had a monopoly on pre-paid "postal cards," which it issued from 1893 in response to a demand for a quick way to send short notes—no emails or texts back then. From 1901, "souvenir cards" became "post cards," and from 1908, you were allowed to write on the back! Before that, the back had been for the address only.

Paper Decorations

Tissue and crepe paper were put to good use to deck out homes and party halls, but once inexpensive, pre-made, diecut decorations became available, these new frills and furbelows quickly became all the rage, although crepe-paper tablecloths, napkins, and streamers remained the norm.

Dennison Manufacturing, which introduced tissue paper and was the first company in America to produce decorative crepe paper, issued its first Hallowe'en products in 1909. The Beistle Company, well-known for its calendars and wooden items (and, strangely enough, feather trees made from chicken feathers dyed green), bought the technology to produce honeycombed tissue paper from Germany in 1910, and chose to make its first seasonal decorations for Hallowe'en. Witches flying past the moon, cats on broomsticks,

bells, lanterns, bats, spiders, and all the other Hallowe'en staples could be unfolded and secured in seconds. Transforming your party venue into a spooky den had never been so quick or easy.

As well as invitations and writing paper, stationery items included gummed seals and stickers, streamers, banners (one Beistle banner of the 1950s was 7 ft/2 m long), place cards, and dance cards. These were folded cards, beautifully inscribed and with silky

tassels, in which, at formal receptions, young ladies could note down which dance they had promised to whom—a delightfully old-fashioned notion in these much more casual times.

These two companies quickly became, and remain, the major manufacturers of novelty decorations made from paper of various types and card stock. Diecut cardboard cutouts of scat cat bands, pumpkins (of course) in various guises, scarecrows, witches, and all the rest were eagerly purchased and no doubt just as readily discarded in a year or so when they became too shabby to put on show any more. Jointed hanging figures were popular—what could be better than a dancing pumpkin head, unless perhaps it was a dancing skeleton?

Vintage Dennison originals are highly collectible, especially gift boxes, novelty paper products, various craft booklets, catalogs, copies of their quarterly magazine, *Parties*, and any of the Dennison "Bogie" books—indispensable if you were throwing a Hallowe'en party in the early 1900s. The first Dennison "Bogie" book was published in 1909, the next one in 1912, and then the books were published annually until the mid-1930s.

Vintage Beistle's ephemera are likewise in demand, so much so that the company has started manufacturing limited numbers of their archived designs. Between the wars, Beistle imported flat-sided paper lanterns from Germany, made with black cardboard strips and transparent orange paper. One 12-panel version from the 1920s is especially sought-after today. Some items from the 1940s and 1950s appeared under the name H.E. Luhrs—the founder's son-in-law who rose to become president of the company—and Beistle originals may bear the diamond trademark, the words "Bee Line," or a flying bee.

COSTUMES AND MASKS

Since at least the 16th century, and probably much longer ago than that, All Hallows' Eve, wherever it has been observed, has involved dressing up.

Mass-produced costumes specifically designed for Hallowe'en first appeared in stores in the 1930s, just as trick-or-treating was getting under way and everyone spent the first part of their party night out on the streets in search of candy and fun. Before then, costumes and masks were mostly homemade and usually just for children. They were supposed to be scary, or of supernatural beings. Often they consisted of not much more than a weird papier-mâché mask, or one drawn on ordinary thick paper or card, tied on with string. Witches, skulls, and spooks were popular, but most were just downright peculiar, depending on the maker's skill, or lack of it, and imagination. Some kids succeeded in looking like latter-day Ned Kellys, but probably not intentionally.

Children would appear in parents' old coats that were too big for them, or wrapped in blankets or rugs. Sheets with cut-out eyes and a painted-on face, possibly of a cat, were not unusual. Party frocks could be embellished with black silhouettes of bats, toads, cats, and witches on broomsticks. The better off who went to formal parties and balls would have had glitzy masks and costumes specially made, but for other folk, improvisation was the key.

Formal Hallowe'en parties in the interwar years often had a fancy-dress theme, such as famous people, with a Hallowe'en twist, which allowed the imagination to run riot. Some featured games, such as bridge and mah jong; others seem to have been less sedate. Perhaps it was easier to let your hair down while costumed and masked, and pretending to be someone else.

Among the first commercially produced costumes, witches, goblins, ghosts, skeletons, and pumpkins reigned supreme, with pirates, clowns, and even mummies getting in on the act. Favorite movie characters, such as Sis Hopkins from the 1919 comedy film of the same name, had already made their appearance. The scarier variety from the increasingly popular horror genre, such as Dracula and Frankenstein's monster, gradually began to turn up on the doorstep, followed by zombies, werewolves, and aliens. Superheroes weren't far behind. In a web posting in 2004, Fred Laurice recalls that, back in 1939, it was customary to wear a costume to school on Hallowe'en, and his mother made him a Superman outfit. (Superman first flew to the rescue in 1938.) The costume was magnificent in blue, red, and yellow, with a big 'S' and a flowing red cape. He was the star of the show, "the happiest kid in the world that Hallowe'en!"

These days it's not just the kids who indulge in fancy dress. The most popular adult themes (according to the National Retail Federation) are witch, pirate, vampire, cat, and clown—so far so traditional, but it doesn't stop there. Each year, among grown-ups and youngsters alike, movie stars, musicians, cartoon characters, and even politicians make their appearance, alongside cowboys, angels, princesses, and whatever else catches the imagination. Traffic lights, ninjas, bananas—anything goes!

If you want to go vintage, stick to traditional witchy and ghostly themes—and pumpkins have never gone out of style. It's fun to make your own costume, but if that's not your skill, or time is short, it's not cheating to buy one in vintage style. An original would be terrific but would probably be expensive.

Candy Containers

In the old days, candy containers, as distinct from trick-or-treating bags, seem to have been as much a part of Hallowe'en décor as a Beistle or Dennison diecut paper cut-out.

On HALLOWEEN You Better Watch Out!

From the 1950s, Rosbro made cute candy containers in hard plastic, mostly in orange and/or black. Some were on wheels. These are not hard to find; prewar candy containers are scarce.

They came in spooky form—witches, black cats, ghosts, devils—or as the inevitable carved pumpkin, and were mostly made of composition (plaster and papier-mâché) or just papier-mâché, but sometimes cardboard or even wood, and usually in Germany or Japan. They often had a lid, in the form of a hat or a head, that could be raised to find the goodies inside. Perhaps these were prizes for the party games. Some containers had wire handles but still seem to have been for inside rather than outside use.

Trick-or-treating bags

These are essentially a postwar creation. Once kids equated the idea of the Hallowe'en holiday with candy, there was no stopping them.

In anticipation of huge numbers of chocolate bars and armfuls of candy corn flowing their way, far too much to carry, some kind of container became necessary, and an ordinary bag would hardly be in the spirit of the occasion. Hence special trick-or-treating bags came into being. These could be made of paper, fabric, or plastic, and naturally they were covered in suitably symbolic designs, featuring all the usual suspects. They came in varying sizes and were mostly elaborately decorated. And if bags were not going to be sturdy enough, ever-hopeful children carried decorated buckets or pails.

pumpkin trick-or-treat bag

In the old days, most Hallowe'en accessories were homemade, so here's a trick-or-treat bucket that's not too difficult to make and will definitely stand out in a crowd. Felt is easy to use, and because it doesn't fray, you won't need to hem it. Raid your button box for green buttons of different sizes and shades, and sew them on securely so they won't get knocked off when the bucket's being enthusiastically swung along and filled to the brim with candy.

You will need

Templates on page 140

Scissors

18 x 12 in. (46 x 30 cm) orange felt

6 x 6 in. (16 x 16 cm) green felt

Pins

Sewing machine

Orange and green sewing thread

Ruler or measuring tape

About 20 green buttons in different sizes

Needle

Pinking shears

1 Using the template on page 140, cut out six segments from orange felt.

2 Again using the template on page 140, cut out six leaf sections from green felt. Pin a leaf shape to an orange felt segment, lining up the top straight edges. Thread your sewing machine with green thread for the top stitching and orange thread for the under stitching, and then machine stitch a leaf to each orange segment. Trim the threads.

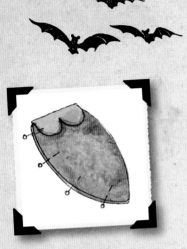

3 With wrong sides together (the right side being the one with the leaf stitched to it), pin and stitch two orange segments together. Trim the threads.

4 In the same way, pin and stitch a third orange segment to one of the orange segments already stitched together. Repeat this with the remaining three segments to make the two halves of the bucket.

5 Pin and stitch the two halves together to form the bucket. Trim the threads.

6 Measure and cut one strip of orange felt 12 x 1⅜ in. (30 x 3.5 cm) and two strips of green felt 12 x ¾ in. (30 x 2 cm). Pin a green strip centrally along the orange strip and machine stitch in place. Trim the threads. Pin and stitch the second green strip to the other side of the orange strip and again machine stitch in place. Then trim the threads.

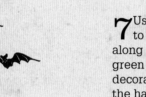

7 Use the pinking shears to cut the orange strip along both sides of the green strips to make a decorative edging along the handle.

8 Pin and stitch one end of the handle to the inside of the felt bucket, stitching a few times to make the handle strong. Stitch the other end of the handle in place directly opposite the first end, again reinforcing the stitches.

9 Hand stitch a few buttons onto each segment of the bucket to decorate.

TEMPLATES

All the templates (except for the Grinning Jack o' Lantern on this page, which is printed at 100%) need to be enlarged by 200% using a photocopier before use.

Grinning Jack o' Lantern
page 66

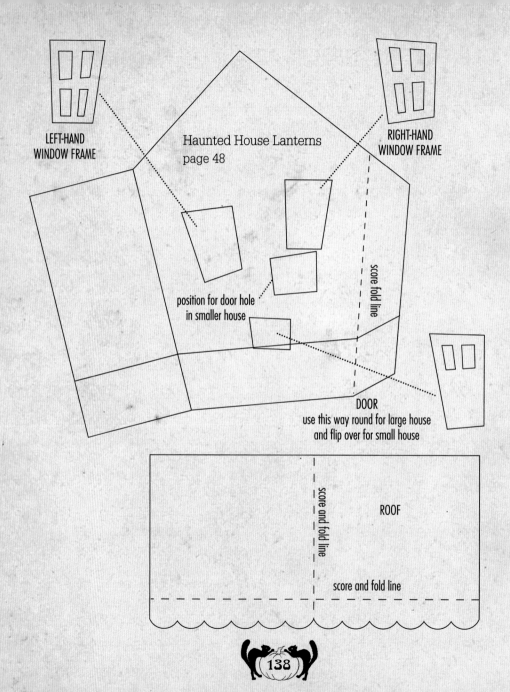

LEFT-HAND
WINDOW FRAME

Haunted House Lanterns
page 48

RIGHT-HAND
WINDOW FRAME

score fold line

position for door hole
in smaller house

DOOR
use this way round for large house
and flip over for small house

score and fold line

ROOF

score and fold line

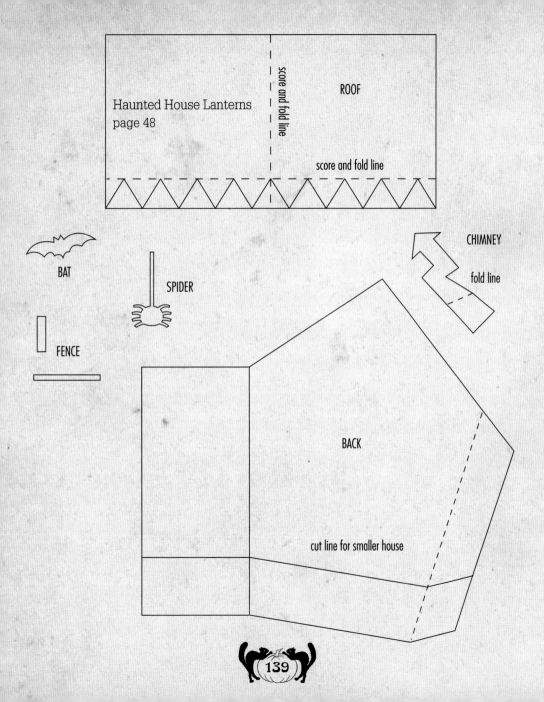

Haunted House Lanterns
page 48

ROOF

score and fold line

score and fold line

BAT

SPIDER

FENCE

CHIMNEY

fold line

BACK

cut line for smaller house

139

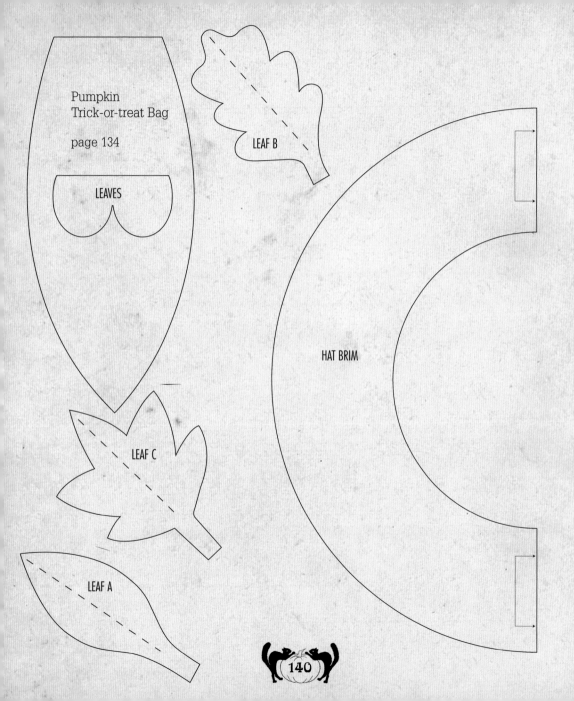

Pumpkin
Trick-or-treat Bag

page 134

LEAVES

LEAF B

LEAF C

LEAF A

HAT BRIM

Witch Costume
page 92

HAT PEAK

INDEX

RESOURCES

The internet is full of information, opinion, and entertainment regarding Hallowe'en, for which I am very grateful. I read many articles and extracts and consulted many websites in researching this book, and found the following particularly helpful:

☆ *The Book of Hallowe'en* Ruth Edna Kelley (Lothrop, Lee and Shepard 1919)

☆ *Bright Ideas for Entertaining* Mrs Herbert B. Linscott (George W. Jacobs, Philadelphia, 9th edition 1905)

☆ *When You Entertain: What To Do, And How* Ida Baily Allen (Coca-Cola Company, Atlanta, 1932)

☆ *The Blue Ribbon Cook Book* Annie Gregory (Monarch Book Company, Chicago, 1901)

☆ *Robert Burns and Friends*, Essays by W. Ormiston Roy Fellows, presented to G. Ross Roy, University of Carolina, 2012, pages 24-37: Footnoted Folklore: Robert Burns' "Hallowe'en" by Corey E. Andrews

☆ "Halloween: A History" Lesley Bannatyne (website article from iskullhalloween.com/hist_article.html)

☆ "Gangsters, Pranksters, and the Invention of Trick-or-Treating, 1930–1960" Samira Kawash, The American Journal of Play volume 4 issue 2/The Strong, New York

☆ The American Folklife Center, Library of Congress, at loc.gov/folklife

☆ The Food Timeline: foodtimeline.org/halloween.html

☆ All About Pumpkins: allaboutpumpkins.com

☆ Colonial Williamsburg: history.org/Foundation/journal/Autumn09/pumpkins.cfm

Stories mentioned on page 95 are available online. Go to americanfolklore.net or themoonlitroad.com for other folktales and ghost stories. You can find out-of-print titles on several websites including gutenberg.org

SUPPLIERS

North America

A.C. Moore
Stores nationwide
1-888-226-6673
www.acmoore.com

Art Supplies Online
800-967-7367
www.artsuppliesonline.com

Craft Site Directory
Useful online resource
www.craftsitedirectory.com

Create For Less
866-333-4463
www.createforless.com

Hobby Lobby
Stores nationwide
1-800-888-0321
shop.hobbylobby.com

Jo-Ann Fabric & Craft Store
Stores nationwide
1-888-739-4120
www.joann.com

Michaels
Stores nationwide
1-800-642-4235
www.michaels.com

S&S Worldwide Craft Supplies
800-288-9941
www.ssww.com

Sunshine Crafts
800-729-2878
www.sunshinecrafts.com

UK suppliers

Early Learning Centre
08705 352 352
www.elc.co.uk

Homecrafts Direct
0116 269 7733
www.homecrafts.co.uk

Hobbycraft
0800 027 2387
www.hobbycraft.co.uk

John Lewis
08456 049 049
www.johnlewis.co.uk

Kidzcraft
01793 327022
www.kidzcraft.co.uk

Paperchase
0161 839 1500 for mail order
www.paperchase.co.uk

Paper and String
www.paper-and-string.co.uk

Try the following websites to be overwhelmed by gorgeous vintage Hallowe'en style:
rubylane.com
countryliving.com
vintagehalloween.com
vintagebeistle.com
etsy.com
pinterest.com

Acknowledgments

Thanks to everyone at CICO for unfailing support and good humor, and in this case especially to Anna Galkina for steering the book through its various stages and finding such lovely illustrations, and Sally Powell for supervising such a brilliant design. Thanks, too, to designer Mark Latter for putting everything together so beautifully.

Of course, this book would never have happened if Cindy Richards hadn't come up with the idea and Gillian Haslam hadn't suggested taking a flyer on me to write it! I'm so pleased and grateful that they did.

The delightful makes are not my doing—thanks to Emma Hardy for those, and to Heather Cameron for the caramel apples.

Last but by no means least, thanks to Rodney for prompting my interest in all things Celtic, and for putting up with old-style Hallowe'en holding sway in our house even though it was Christmas at the time!